T0034118

FRENCH COOKING IN TEN MINUTES

Translated by
Philip and Mary Hyman
North Point Press
Farrar, Straus and Giroux
New York

FRENCH COOKING IN TEN MINUTES

O R

Adapting to the Rhythm of Modern Life

(1930)

B Y

EDOUARD de POMIANE

North Point Press
A division of Farrar, Straus and Giroux
18 West 18th Street, New York 10011

Translation and introduction copyright © 1977
by Farrar, Straus and Giroux, Inc.
All rights reserved
Distributed in Canada by Douglas & McIntyre Ltd.
Printed in the United States of America
Originally published by Editions Paul Martial, France
Published in 1977 in the United States by Farrar, Straus and Giroux
First North Point Press edition, 1994

Library of Congress Cataloging-in-Publication Data
Pomiane, Edouard de, 1875–1964.
    [Cuisine en dix minutes. English]
    French cooking in ten minutes : or, Adapting to the rhythm of modern life
(1950) / By Edouard de Pomiano [i.e. E. A. Pozerski]; [translated by Philip
and Mary Hyman].
        p.   cm.
    Translation of La cuisine en dix minutes.
    Includes index.
    ISBN-13: 978-0-86547-480-2
    ISBN-10: 0-86547-480-x
    1. Cookery, French.   2. Quick and easy cookery.   3. Menus.   I. Title.

TX719 .P74513 1994
641.5944—dc21

                                                                96222776

Designed by Cynthia Krupat

www.fsgbooks.com

26

The pen-and-ink drawings that appear throughout this book were done
by André Giroux for the original 1930 edition.

I dedicate this book to
Madame X, asking for ten minutes
of her kind attention.
Edouard de Pomiane
1930

CONTENTS

INTRODUCTION

(1)

When Edouard de Pomiane died in 1964 at the age of
ninety, he was one of the most highly respected and
widely read cooks in France—and yet he was neither a
cook nor French. Edouard Pomian Pozerski was born,
true enough, in Paris, but he always felt strongly attached
to Poland, the country his parents had only recently left.
Even though the family name was changed to "de
Pomiane" when they settled in France, their Polish
ancestry was a source of pride, especially to the young
Edouard. He was legally French, but considered him-
self Polish and only an "adopted" Frenchman. His
foreign origin made him more eclectic than many of his
French contemporaries and may account for the variety
and originality of his cookbooks when they are compared
to the more traditional French books of the same period.
So our assertion that Pomiane was not French is only
partially true. And what about not being a cook? Well,
here too some explanations have to be made. Dr.
Pomiane, as he was known officially, was in fact a doctor
of medicine and a research scientist at the prestigious
Pasteur Institute in Paris. His interest in cooking started

while he was working on a chemical analysis of the fermenting juices of the stomach. He soon became interested in the composition of various foods and, finally, in the process that transformed these raw materials into substances acceptable to the stomach—in other words, *cooking*. He combined his interest in the scientific and the sensual in a study which he christened "Gastrotechnology." His success as a cook, and as a teacher of cooking, stemmed not only from his scientific approach to the basic culinary processes but from his good taste and appreciation for all those unknown elements that personalize the execution of any recipe. Cooking was always considered an art by Pomiane.

Dr. Pomiane became an active lecturer on food and a teacher of cooking while continuing his work at the Pasteur Institute. During the 1930's he was particularly well known for a series of radio programs in which he gave his audience recipes and told amusing stories about his own experiences in the kitchen. In the course of his life he wrote twenty-two books on cooking, all of which contained a characteristic mixture of personal anecdotes and precise information about food. His personality, good humor, and professionally exacting attitude toward his recipes made these books popular, and their author became a celebrity in the Paris culinary world. So, to say that Pomiane was not a cook is like saying he wasn't French—another half-truth.

A book on ten-minute cooking seems logical today, now that microwave ovens and deep freezers have revolutionized the prepared-food market. But in 1930, when this book was written, the ten-minute cook didn't have nearly as many time-savers at his disposal, and the challenge of preparing excellent meals in such a short period of time was much greater. The subtitle of this book is "Adapting to the Rhythm of Modern Life." Almost fifty years have passed since these words were written, and since life in 1930 was calm compared to the speed of life today, the book is more useful now than ever before. Pomiane tried to cushion the jolts of our accelerated existence by making hurriedly prepared meals not just "fast food" but delicious food as well.

A few things have to be understood about French meals and French cooking in general in order to fully appreciate Pomiane's work. The book begins with a series of menus which may look complex and difficult to prepare. Any one of them, however, can be prepared in ten minutes *if* the cook is well organized. More importantly, these menus give the cook an idea of the variety of things he can prepare in a very short time and serve in a four- or five-course meal. "Courses" are essential to French cooking; no one in France would sit down to a main dish *only* and consider that his dinner. This isn't because the French are big eaters. Eating several *small* courses rather than one or two large ones usually makes the meal not only more varied and nourishing but less fattening as well. The key to successfully executing any one of these menus is the French emphasis on the quality of each dish rather than the quantity.

Pomiane assumes that his reader has acquired the French habit of accompanying each meal with both wine and bread. The wine is optional—drink water if you must, not a soft drink!—but the bread is essential. A

French- or Italian-style loaf, eaten sparingly during dinner and used, in the best French tradition, to soak up the sauce you've prepared, will make your dinner more enjoyable. Ask for advice where you buy wine and, if possible, serve French wine with French food.

Pomiane also assumes that all good Frenchmen know how to appreciate cheese, which is mentioned in almost every one of his menus. It's always served *after* the main dish and should be accompanied by a slice of bread and a glass of wine. Don't take this cheese course for granted; it will add a lot to the variety and value of your meal. Any cheese will do—Swiss or Cheddar are fine, but try soft cheeses like Brie or Camembert for a change.

A few last words about the menus: You'll notice that a green salad is *never* served at the beginning of the meal —it always comes after the main dish and before cheese and dessert. This is another French custom that's worth a try. A simple green salad is especially refreshing at this point in the meal. By "simple" we mean a small salad of lettuce leaves only in an oil-and-vinegar dressing. You'll also notice that several menus list fruit instead of dessert. Despite the French talent for pastries, a typical family meal in France is more likely to end with fresh fruit. The menus' mixture of raw and cooked foods is healthy and refreshing. Don't try to cut corners by leaving out a course. The French have the right idea: Bread, a tossed salad, a slice of cheese, and some fresh fruit go a long way toward completing your meal and making it more enjoyable. And you haven't lost a second of your ten-minute cooking time!

(2)

French Cooking in Ten Minutes was written for both
the novice and the experienced cook. Even the best cooks
are often baffled when faced with only a short period of
time in which to prepare an entire meal. Pomiane goes to
great lengths to explain the problems involved in this
kind of cooking, and the reader will surely benefit from
reading the book from start to finish. One recipe is often
the starting point from which many others can be im-
provised, and the basic cooking techniques explained
in the beginning of the book should be thoroughly understood.

Despite Pomiane's elaborate introduction, some addi-
tional comments are now necessary. In the almost fifty
years since this book was written certain changes have
been made that Pomiane couldn't foresee. For example,
there is no mention of frozen food in the course of this
work. When precooked foods are called for, canned
goods are always used. This was logical enough in 1930,
when canned goods were the only widely available form
of processed foods, but today frozen foods are just as
good, if not better in many cases, and can usually be
considered replacements for their canned equivalent. But
when Pomiane calls for something *fresh*, don't use a
canned or frozen substitute unless the product simply
isn't available in any other form. Pomiane *prefers* fresh
foods to processed ones whenever there is time enough
for their use.

Pomiane occasionally uses non-processed but prepared

foods. All over France are little shops called "char-
cuteries" where food is prepared on the premises and sold
either as carry-out "hot plates" or as individual items to
be eaten as they are or reheated at home. These shops
specialize in pork products—especially sausages and
patés—but also sell a variety of vegetable salads, cold
cuts, etc. In this translation we refer the American reader
to delicatessens for many of the prepared foods the
Frenchman would normally find in his local charcuterie.
Some of the products mentioned can also be found at
specialty food shops.

Problems might be encountered in the chapter devoted
to the use of vegetable flours. Some of these flours are
available in specialty shops, but if you can't find them
and want to make the vegetable purees Pomiane de-
scribes, try using canned cream soups, very lightly diluted
with milk or water.

Pomiane neglects to mention the substitution of leftovers for canned (or frozen) goods. When you cook fresh
vegetables (potatoes or green beans for example), be sure
to prepare a little extra and use these leftovers instead of
their canned or frozen counterparts in Pomiane's recipes.
The same applies to meat: a chicken roasted on Sunday
can be made into two ten-minute meals later on in the
week. If you ever go so far as to prepare your own "pot au
feu," you'll have real meat bouillon to use instead of
bouillon cubes.

One last word about ingredients—whenever wine is
called for in cooking Pomiane always means French
wines. They needn't be the most expensive vintages,
but stick to dry white wines (like Muscadet or Gros Plant)

or French red Burgundies or Côtes du Rhône. Don't use
either sweet white or sweet red wine in any case.

(3)

Pomiane's insistence on the use of a gas stove in ten-
minute cooking is somewhat anachronistic. In 1930 electric stoves were virtually unknown and those that existed
were extremely primitive. Gas is in many cases still pref-
erable today because it heats so quickly, but modern
electric stoves aren't to be ignored; Pomiane might very
well have preferred them for some things had he written
his book thirty years later. This brings us to some comments about the gas stove Pomiane uses. Remember,
back in 1930 coal stoves were still common and gas stoves
were usually small substitutes designed for apartment-
house living. Pomiane assumes, for example, that you
will have only two, maybe three, burners at your disposal. Don't be confused when he alludes to these minia-
ture machines, which are still common in France. Just
be grateful that your stove is probably larger and more
efficient than anything Pomiane knew.

The fact that electrical appliances in general—blend-
ers, grinders, etc.—aren't mentioned in Pomiane's book is
another indication of the book's age. Use these appliances
whenever you can and you might continue to reduce the
cooking time; Pomiane would certainly have approved.
But one modern invention he probably would have
frowned on is the non-stick frying pan. These pans might
be used for omelets or crepes, but *never* for pan-frying
meat or fish. It's essential that the food *stick* to the bottom

of the pan (at least a little) if you're going to make a sauce in the same pan. The flavor the food releases in cooking is recovered in the sauces.

Otherwise, the basic kitchen utensils Pomiane lists at the beginning of the book haven't changed much in the last fifty years.

In closing, a few words should be added about the occasional vagueness of Pomiane's recipes. The ingredients were not listed separately before each recipe in the original French edition. Although we've done so here when we thought it would be helpful, we haven't added specific information where none was given in the original book, so a recipe might call for fresh herbs or tomato paste without specifying the exact amount. This was Pomiane's intention. He'll hint at the amount he uses (e.g., adding "a little" of something, or working a sauce until a certain color or texture appears), but in many cases exact measurements aren't given because *your* taste will be the deciding factor. Experimentation is a necessary part of perfecting any recipe; if you stay within the limits Pomiane implies, you can't go wrong.

Note: Italics indicate that a recipe for the dish appears elsewhere in the book.

Philip and Mary Hyman

PREFACE

I am neither crazy nor a micromaniac. (A micromaniac is someone obsessed with reducing things to their smallest possible form. This word, by the way, is not in the dictionary.) Yet I was called an irresponsible fool the day my book *La Cuisine en six leçons* came out. How could I possibly teach someone French cooking in only six lessons, when most people assume that it takes at least ten years to become a good cook? I had foreseen this criticism, and in the preface to that book I tried to show how a scientific approach could radically shorten the time spent in learning any new discipline, including cooking. I thought I had shown that I was fully conscious of "speeding" and was not simply ignoring the element of time.

In this book I will explain how you can prepare dinner in ten minutes. Since ten minutes is such a small amount of time as to be almost no time at all, I will surely be called a micromaniac.

I won't go on trying to explain or defend myself; I will simply show you how many wonderful dishes you can prepare in ten minutes. The only condition for making them is that you must live in a town where you can buy everything you need. Obviously, if you have to catch your trout in a mountain stream before you can prepare it, it will take you a lot longer than ten minutes, even if you just sprinkle it with salt and eat it raw.

I am writing this book for students, dressmakers, secretaries, artists, lazy people, poets, men of action, dreamers, scientists, and everyone else who has only an hour for lunch or dinner but still wants thirty minutes of peace to enjoy a cup of coffee.

Modern life is so hectic that we sometimes feel as if time is going up in smoke. But we don't want that to happen to our steak or omelet, so let's hurry. Ten minutes is enough. One minute more and all will be lost.

Edouard de Pomiane

FRENCH
COOKING
IN TEN
MINUTES

SOME INDISPENSABLE CONCEPTS FOR UNDERSTANDING THIS BEAUTIFUL BOOK

First of all, let me tell you that this is a beautiful book. I can say that because this is its first page. I just sat down to write it, and I feel happy, the way I feel whenever I start a new project.

My pen is full of ink, and there's a stack of paper in front of me. I love this book because I'm writing it for you. It's nice to imagine that I'll be able to let my pen go and you'll understand everything it writes down. My ideas run on faster and faster—I'll be able to say everything in less than ten minutes.

My book won't even be ten pages long . . . It's going to be ridiculous . . . Worse than that, it will be incomprehensible.

A more scientific approach will make things clearer, so I'll start by telling you everything you should know before you start ten-minute cooking, even if all you're going to do is boil an egg.

The first thing you must do when you get home, before you take off your coat, is go to the kitchen and light the stove. It will have to be a gas stove, because otherwise you'll never be able to cook in ten minutes.

Next, fill a pot large enough to hold a quart of water. Put it on the fire, cover it, and bring it to a boil. What's the water for? I don't know, but it's bound to be good

for something, whether in preparing your meal or just making coffee. If you're planning to deep fry anything, put a pot half filled with lard or cooking oil on another burner.

All this should be done immediately, because the time necessary to heat the water or fat shouldn't count in the ten minutes it takes to cook your meal. Now that everything's started, you can take off your coat and start cooking.

Food can be cooked by (1) boiling, (2) deep frying, (3) broiling, or (4) braising. This last technique is virtually useless in ten-minute cooking because it is a very long, slow process. Many of the dishes French cooking is famous for are prepared in this way, but they simply can't be done if you're in a hurry. So we'll just consider the first three cooking methods.

Boiling

To cook quickly by this method, drop the ingredients into rapidly boiling water. You will find some bubbling away on your stove.

You will generally be able to cook only small things— noodles or dumplings, for example—because you want them to cook quickly. But you can also cook a 14-ounce piece of beef or lamb rapidly in this way. Unfortunately, you won't be able to boil fresh vegetables; they just won't cook through in the limited amount of time we're dealing with.

In sum, to boil something, you simply drop it into boiling water, add salt, then cover the pot. As soon as the water stars boiling again, take the top off the pot so you can see what's happening inside. You will be able to save time by knowing immediately when the food is done and should be taken off the heat.

Deep Frying

Food cooks at around 212° Fahrenheit in boiling water, but deep frying requires a temperature of about 230°. This is why the fat or oil in the deep fryer must be heated well in advance. You will know when it is ready because it will start smoking. As soon as you see the first signs of smoke rising from the surface of the fat, you must *immediately* drop whatever you want to fry into it. If you wait, the fat will get too hot, burn, and begin to decompose. If this happens, it will have to be thrown away. By dropping food into it, you will lower the temperature of the fat. If this is done at just the right moment, you will not only be using the fat at its best temperature but you will keep it from burning and so be able to use it again another time.

Only small, thin portions of food can be deep fried, such as small fish or sliced potatoes. They must be absolutely dry before being dropped into the hot fat, otherwise the water will be converted into steam and the fat will splatter. If this happens, watch out for your clothes, and make sure the fat in the pot doesn't catch on fire. If it does, don't panic—it's not at all serious. Simply cover the pot with its top or a thick towel and the fire will go out. If you want to fry something that cannot be dried off easily, such as a fish, roll it in flour; that way the outside will be dry and the fish will fry nicely without splattering.

Once the fish is coated with flour, heat the fat until it begins to smoke, drop your fish into it, and let it cook for about 5 minutes. Take the fish out, turn up the heat as high as possible, and when the fat starts smoking again, drop the fish back into the pot and let it cook 2 minutes longer. Now take it out and let the fat drain off. Sprinkled with salt, it's ready to eat, but be careful not to burn your mouth.

Broiling

Meat can be excellent broiled; all you have to do is grease it lightly with oil or melted butter before you expose it to the heat. But what exactly is broiling, anyway? Let's use a little logic and see if that gives us the answer.

In order for a lamb chop to be well broiled and delicious, it has to be nicely browned on the outside but tender and juicy on the inside. In order to keep the juices inside the lamb chop, you obviously have to do something to keep them from seeping out. It doesn't take much of a genius to figure that out, and if you know a little basic chemistry, it will be easier to see what you have to do and why.

To keep the juices from seeping out, the surface of your lamb chop will have to be hardened—that is, transformed into an impermeable shell, so to speak. That's simple enough. Meat contains albumin, and albumin coagulates and hardens under the effects of heat. Since you want this albumin to harden rapidly, you will have to expose it to a very hot flame.

So if you want to broil something, light your broiler as soon as you walk in the door, at the same time you put your pot of water on the fire, before taking off your coat and hat.

As soon as the broiler is hot, place the buttered meat on a grill and slide it under the flame. Let it cook 5 minutes. Turn it over and let it cook 5 minutes more. Salt and serve. Unless you have a tiny grill, you can broil four lamb chops at once.

Roasting

You will never be able to roast anything in ten minutes. Not in the oven, on a spit, or in a pot. But if you have a small piece of meat, you can "roast" it in a frying pan. The frying pan is something you will use very often in ten-minute cooking. You can cook meat, fish, vegetables, fruit, eggs, and quick desserts in it, so we'll stop a minute and talk a little about pan-frying.

Pan-Frying

Everything that's been said about deep frying and broiling applies to pan-frying. When you put butter or fat into the frying pan, don't put your steak into the pan until the fat starts to smoke. As in broiling, whatever you cook in a pan should have a nice crust on the outside, so your frying pan should be extremely hot. You must put it on the hottest flame possible, but in order not to smell up the kitchen too much, it's a good idea to open the window.

When your steak is nicely browned on one side, turn

it over, and when it looks brown on the other side, turn down the fire and add salt. When the meat is done, take it out of the pan; stuck on the bottom of the frying pan you'll see the caramelized albumin and sugars left by the meat. This is what cooks calls a glaze.

This glaze is dissolved by pouring liquid into the frying pan. When the liquid boils, the caramel dissolves, making a delicious sauce. A great many sauces can be made in this way, depending on the liquid you use. Water, white wine, port, Madeira, cognac, beer, bouillon, red wine are only a few examples. Just think of the fabulous things you'll be able to make!

Thickening with Flour

If you like smooth, creamy sauces, you have to thicken them. One way to do this is to add flour to your sauce,

but to do it correctly, certain basic—and logical—rules
have to be followed.

Starch thickens sauces because, when it comes into
contact with water and heat, it forms a paste. If you
throw a handful of flour into your sauce, the flour will
stick together and your sauce will be not only watery
but lumpy as well. To make a successful sauce, here's
what you must do.

In the frying pan which contains the meat glaze, place
a small lump of butter. Add a teaspoon of flour. With a
fork, mix the flour and butter together; then wait until
the mixture turns golden brown. You have just made a
"roux." Now, little by little, add the liquid you want to
use in making your sauce—it should be cold when you
add it. Heat the sauce slowly, stirring all the time. The
starch in the flour will turn to paste when you begin
adding the liquid, and at first your sauce will be very
thick. Just keep adding liquid slowly until the sauce is
the consistency you want it to be, then stop pouring and
bring the sauce to a boil. Let it bubble about 5 seconds—
now it's ready.

Thickening with Egg

Sauces can also be thickened by adding one or more egg
yolks to them. But this can be tricky, so you must be
very careful. I'll tell you why: mixed with a liquid, egg
yolk starts to thicken when it is exposed to a temperature
of about 145° Fahrenheit, but if it is heated much more
than that, the yolk will begin to harden; it will coagulate,
and the sauce will "separate" and be spoiled. To avoid

this, the egg yolk should be added only to sauces that are lukewarm. Once it has been added, stir constantly and place your saucepan on a medium fire. From time to time, test the temperature of the sauce with your finger, and when it becomes too hot to stand, turn the heat down and wait for the sauce to thicken. Don't expect it to thicken too much, and don't stop stirring . . . the result could be catastrophic. The sauce will get thicker as you stir it and as it cools.

These are the basic rules that must be followed in ten-minute cooking, and anyone who wants to cook at all must know them.

SOME ADVICE
AND SAMPLE
MENUS

Cooking Utensils

Since you will be spending a minimum of time cooking, your kitchen doesn't have to look like a showroom of cooking utensils. All the equipment you need can be kept in a small cupboard and taken out only when necessary. Here's what you will need:

A series of saucepans, ranging from 5 to 9 inches in diameter

A 4½-inch enameled saucepan

Two frying pans that are *absolutely flat on the bottom, not warped.* One should measure 6½ inches across the bottom, the other 7½ inches

A shallow, fireproof dish made of porcelain or metal

A kettle large enough to hold a quart of water

A colander

A deep fryer, or a pot with a wire basket that fits into it

A funnel

A ladle
A skimmer or a slotted spoon
A wire skimmer for deep frying
A wire whisk
Two wooden spatulas
A large kitchen knife
A paring knife
Some ordinary stainless-steel knives, forks, and spoons
Three bowls
One salad bowl
A coffee pot with a filter, large enough to make two
    cups of coffee (or two individual filters that fit over
    the cups)
A coffee grinder

Since the saucepans and frying pans fit into each
other, you can store them neatly inside your cabinet. The

only thing that really takes up space is your deep fryer. If you use oil for deep frying, wait until it cools off, then pour it through a funnel into a large bottle or jar, and keep it in the cabinet too. The spoons, knives, ladle, skimmers, and spatulas will fit into a drawer.

If you want to decorate your kitchen with appetizing pictures, it is best to frame them under glass so the grease from cooking doesn't spoil them.

When you're cooking, be sure to open the window as often as you can, and once a week sponge off the kitchen walls with a little soapy water. That way, your kitchen will be a spotlessly clean laboratory that you will transform, I'm sure, into an artist's studio.

Some Luncheon Menus

Noodles Czechoslovakian style
Rib steak with onions
Cucumbers with sour cream
Cheese
Fruit salad

Smoked haddock English style
Veal scallops Zingara
Green salad
Coeur à la crème
Fruit

Hot boiled shrimp
Fried sausage patties
Green-pea puree
Cheese
Fruit

Poached eggs with black butter
Fried veal scallops
Green peas
Green salad with cream dressing
Cheese
Fruit

Smoked sausage and olives
Loin lamb chops
Sautéed potatoes
Green salad
Cheese
Chocolate éclairs

Burgundy snails
Quail à la crapaudine
Asparagus salad
Cheese
Fruit

Tripe à la mode de Caen
Green peas with ham
Green salad
Coeur à la crème with pineapple

Scrambled eggs with truffles
Venison cutlets
Chestnut puree
Green salad
Cheese
Fruit

Skate with black butter
Green beans with sour cream
Potato salad
Cheese
Fruit

Mussels with saffron
Buttered spinach
Tomato salad
Omelet flambé
Fruit

Some Dinner Menus

Ham soup
Filet steaks Dauphinois
Buttered peas
Cheese
Mocha cookies

Saint-Germain soup
Veal cutlets Pojarski
Beet salad
Cheese
Fruit salad

Semolina soup
Pork chops with sauerkraut
Green salad
Omelet flambé
Cheese
Fruit

Onion soup
Saddle of hare with sour cream
Buttered beets
Green salad
Cheese
Jam cookies

Beet soup
Larks en cocotte
Sautéed green beans
Cheese
Coeur à la crème with jam

Soup à la Grecque
Cold chicken with mayonnaise
Tomatoes Polish style
Cheese
Cream of chestnuts

Sorrel soup
Wiener schnitzel
Baby limas in cream sauce
Green salad
Cheese
Fruit

Velouté soup with tarragon
Chicken sautéed with mushrooms
Green salad
Cheese
Cream puff

Cream of mushroom soup
Frankfurter sausages
Potato salad
Cheese
Coeur à la crème

Pumpkin soup
Creamed salt cod
Buttered green peas
Cheese
Fruit

Esau soup
Veal cutlets Milanese
French-fried potatoes
Green salad
Cheese
Fruit

Scampi à l'Américaine
Filet steaks Rossini
Asparagus salad
Cheese
Fruit

A Few Words on How to Behave at the Table

Don't misunderstand me—I'm not a professor of etiquette, and you have excellent table manners, of course. But my experience in having guests to dinner, and being the host, conversationalist, cook, maid, carver, and wine steward, all at once, prompts me to give you a little helpful advice. You have just looked at a list of menus, each of which is composed of several quickly prepared courses. Nothing takes more than ten minutes to make. But unless you organize yourself so that the various preparations

overlap, it will take you half an hour to cook three dishes.

Let's not forget that you can cook at least two things at once, since your stove has at least two burners. Therefore, the third course should be, if at all possible, something you can reheat. You will be able to do this over a very low flame while you are eating the first two courses. So always try to compose menus with a third course that can cook without your being there to watch it. Don't make sautéed potatoes, for example; reheat some green peas or sauerkraut instead. In order to have as pleasant and as elegant a dinner as possible, *do your best to avoid running back and forth between the kitchen and the dining room.* Have a little table within arm's reach of the dining-room table, and keep the knives, forks, and plates for the different courses there, as well as the cheese and your dessert. As the meal progresses, change the plates and cutlery, putting the dirty ones on the little side table.

Each time you go to the kitchen (you should never make more than two trips), take with you as many dirty dishes as you can, so that, by dessert, your side table is completely clean. While serving, don't let your guest help you, as that would only cause chaos and confusion, which would be bad for your digestion. Have him stay at the table, and if he's enjoying what he's eating, he won't even notice that you've left him alone for a minute.

Organizing the Meal

Let's say that you have planned the following menu for lunch:

Cheese omelet
Veal scallop with green peas
Green salad
Cheese
Fruit
Coffee

Are you going to prepare these dishes one after the other, as they are listed on the menu? No, because if you did, your lunch would be a dismal failure.

As soon as you get home:

1. Put a large pot of water on the heat, and cover it (this is an unchanging ritual).

2. Open a can of green peas, and pour the contents into a bowl. Put it aside.

3. Beat the eggs in another bowl; add salt and grated cheese. Put it aside.

4. Place some washed lettuce leaves in a salad bowl. Add oil, vinegar, salt, and pepper, but don't mix it up. Put it aside.

5. Grind up the coffee, and place it in the coffee filter. Put it aside.

6. Put a lump of butter into a frying pan, and when it smokes, brown your scallop of veal, first on one side, then on the other. Eight minutes is enough. Add the peas, but not their juice, and leave the pan on very low heat.

7. Take the pot of water off the heat, and put some butter in your other frying pan. When it smokes, add the eggs, and make your omelet; that will take about 3 minutes.

Sit down at the table and eat your omelet while the peas are heating up. Then the veal will be ready—golden brown served on a jade-green carpet. Put the pot of water back on the fire.

Mix the salad and eat it, then eat some Brie cheese, delicious with a little butter.

Before you peel your orange, pour 2 cups of boiling water over the ground coffee in the filter above the coffee pot; the coffee will make itself while you eat your fruit.

Now everything's done . . . or should I say, now everything can begin. Put the coffee pot on the burner for 20 seconds, but make sure the coffee doesn't boil, whatever you do. Pour a little boiling water into your coffee cup, then throw the water out. Fill your cup with the hot coffee. Lean back in your armchair and put your feet up. Light a cigarette. Take a nice long puff, then blow the smoke to the ceiling. Enjoy the coffee's aroma, take a long sip. Close your eyes. Think about that second puff, that second sip—you're rich!

In the background, the radio's playing a tango or some jazz.

Of course, if there are two of you for lunch, you'll need two veal scallops, two cups of coffee, two cigarettes. Still, ten minutes is enough time to prepare the main dish. With two of you, though, I suggest you drink your coffee in the dining room, with your elbows on the table. Talk to each other, but don't dream, because your lunch hour will disappear in no time. You have just enough time to eat your meal, and not much more to digest it.

If you plan to have soup, always remember to prepare it first, with the water boiling on the stove. Soup takes longer than anything else to prepare, and it's the first course to be served, so you don't want to waste any time.

UNVARIED
HORS D'OEUVRES

You won't be able to make complicated hors d'oeuvres. You have no right to, since you don't have the time. In any case, their only purpose is to keep you from starving before the main dish is brought out. So use them sparingly.

If you like hors d'oeuvres more than anything else, stick up for yourself and make a whole meal composed of nothing but these small delights. Then the cooking you do will be reduced to almost nothing—except the coffee.

So go to the local delicatessen, if there is one, or to a well-stocked supermarket and pick up some salami, tuna-fish salad, olives, mushroom salad, and 3 slices of prosciutto (country ham). Add a little butter, some Roquefort cheese, and some fruit, and you'll be happy.

But don't make this type of meal too often; it will ruin your health. You'll probably get tired of it, anyway.

There's no reason, though, why you shouldn't start a meal with a few things to nibble on. Just don't eat an egg course as well. You can eat your tuna fish or 2 sardines while your pork chop is sizzling on the stove with some chestnut puree. Don't eat sardines unless there are two of you, because even though the can looks small, there's too much in it for one person.

When they're in season, red radishes, eaten with a little butter, make an excellent hors d'oeuvre, as do black radishes, cut into slices and seasoned with cream, salt, and vinegar. Tomato salad is very refreshing, and sliced beets, served with sour cream, are delicious.

A favorite English hors d'oeuvre consists of celery sticks dipped in mustard. Or, if you would like an Oriental flavor, try some black olives and smoked sprats after a little glass of Greek mastic or raki and a big glass of water.

Only a millionaire can afford black caviar, and millionaires are not very interested in ten-minute cooking, but for the rest of us, there's red caviar. A 2-ounce serving of it costs little more than a can of sardines. Eat it on some slices of buttered bread, sprinkled with a few drops of lemon juice.

One slice of prosciutto won't break the bank. If it is

cured to perfection, it will literally melt in your mouth. Eat it with buttered bread. An uncooked slice of Canadian bacon, sprinkled with a little paprika also makes an excellent hors d'oeuvre.

No one, except maybe your doctor, would tell you that you shouldn't start your lunch with half a dozen fresh oysters, opened for you by the man who sells them. Eat them with a slice of buttered brown bread and a few drops of lemon juice, accompanied by a glass of cold, very dry, white wine.

You can make a whole lunch of oysters if you eat them the way they do in Bordeaux. Buy a dozen oysters. Fry some sausages. Take a bite of burning hot sausage, then soothe your mouth with a cool oyster. Twelve times . . . a coffee, and there you are.

Try not to eat a green salad at the start of a meal. You'll eat too much because you're hungry, then five minutes later you'll be sorry you did.

I've really said too much about hors d'oeuvres. I meant to prescribe them in tiny doses. If you're not convinced, do as you like. After all, that's the best way to enjoy what you're eating.

SUPER-QUICK
SOUPS

Can a soup be prepared in ten minutes? Certainly, if you follow a few guidelines. The longest part is bringing 2 cups of water to a boil. But that time doesn't count, since before we started cooking we put a pot full of water on the stove. Here are about twenty soups, all of which can be prepared quickly.

Beef Bouillon

No. Beef bouillon cannot be prepared from scratch in ten minutes.

But you can buy tablets, cubes, or liquid meat extract which make bouillon when dissolved in water. Some of them are detestable. They are not made from meat at all but result from the action of hydrochloric acid on casein and blood serum. They are very inexpensive, but gastronomically worthless. On the other hand, there are products made by boiling beef for hours in water. All of the nutritive juices pass from the meat into the water, making a bouillon which is then reduced over a high heat. Depending upon whether the water in it is allowed to evaporate completely or only partially, either a solid paste or a syrupy liquid is obtained. Some of these products are excellent. Use whichever one you like.

In order to make beef bouillon, pour 2 cups of boiling water into a pot. Add 2 bouillon cubes, or if you prefer, 2 teaspoons of liquid meat extract. Let it boil a few seconds. Add salt if needed, and a small pat of butter. When the butter has melted, pour the soup into teacups and serve.

Semolina Soup

Make 2 cups of *beef bouillon* following the preceding recipe. When it boils, add 2 tablespoons of very finely ground semolina, stirring constantly. As soon as the soup comes to a boil again, turn the heat down and let it boil gently for 7 or 8 minutes more. It's ready. Serve it in two soup plates.

Ham Soup

Make 2 cups of *semolina soup*. While it's cooking, chop up a slice of ham as finely as possible. Just before serving, add the ham to the soup. Give it a stir, let it boil for 2 seconds, and serve.

Soup à la Grecque

Make 2 cups of *semolina soup*. When it has finished cooking, take the pot off the stove. Break an egg, and separate the white from the yolk. Place the yolk in a bowl, and stir into it a tablespoon of hot soup. When well mixed, add 2 more tablespoons of soup, stir, then pour the contents of the bowl into the pot of soup. Mix together well, then add the juice of a quarter of a lemon. Serve immediately, before the soup cools off.

Velouté Soup

Prepare 2 cups of *beef bouillon* and bring to a boil. Place a tablespoon of potato starch in a bowl and dilute it with a little cold water. Pour the contents of the bowl into the boiling bouillon, stirring constantly. Let the soup boil on low heat for 5 minutes, then take the pot off the stove.

Now put 2 egg yolks in a small serving bowl. Stir in 2 tablespoons of hot bouillon, and when well mixed, add 2 more tablespoons. Stirring constantly, add the rest of the bouillon, and the soup is ready to serve.

Velouté Soup with Tarragon

Make 2 cups of *velouté soup*. When ready to serve, add some fresh tarragon leaves.

Parmesan Soup

Prepare 2 cups of *beef bouillon*. Put a few small pieces of stale bread, or toast, into two soup bowls, pour the bouillon over them, sprinkle the soup with grated Parmesan cheese, and serve.

Beet Soup

Make 2 cups of *beef bouillon* and bring it to a boil.

Take ¼ pound of cooked beets. Peel them if necessary, rinse them off, and chop them up very fine.

Put the beets into the bouillon and let the soup boil for 3 minutes. Then add a teaspoonful of good wine vinegar. Let the soup boil just a second or two longer, then pour it through a strainer into your soup bowls. Throw away the beet pulp. The bouillon will be a beautiful deep red.

You can serve this soup in two ways: just as it is, or with a tablespoon of sour cream added to each bowl just before serving.

Cream of Mushroom Soup

2 cups beef bouillon
1 tbsp. barley meal
3 heaping tbsp. dried
  mushrooms

4 tbsp. heavy cream

Prepare 2 cups of *beef bouillon*. While it's boiling, put the barley meal into a bowl and dilute it with a little cold water. Pour it into the bouillon, stirring constantly. Add the dried mushrooms, and let the soup boil for 10 minutes, or better yet, 15 minutes; please forgive me.

Strain the soup into a bowl and throw away the mushrooms. Add the heavy cream to the soup, and serve.

Onion Soup

Butter
1 large onion, chopped fine
1 tsp. flour
Boiling water
Salt and pepper

Stale bread, or toast
Grated Parmesan cheese
Hot milk, cream, or 1 beaten
  egg (all optional)

Place some butter in a frying pan, and when it begins to smoke, add the onion. Cook over a very hot fire until the onion is a nice mahogany brown. Add the flour, stir it in well, then moisten the mixture with a little warm water. Add enough boiling water to bring the total amount of liquid to 2 cups. Now pour the soup into a pot. Bring it back to a boil, and let it cook for 8 minutes; then add salt and pepper to taste. In a serving bowl, place some small pieces of stale bread, or toast, and sprinkle grated Parmesan cheese over them. Add the soup and serve.

Just after you have poured the soup into the serving bowl, you can add, if you like, a little hot milk, some cream, or a beaten egg.

Sorrel Soup

Butter	2 tbsp. finely ground
2 oz. (a large handful) of	semolina
sorrel leaves	Salt
2 cups boiling water	4 tbsp. heavy cream

Melt a lump of butter in a saucepan. Add the sorrel leaves, and stir over the heat. The sorrel will melt down into a sort of paste. Now add the boiling water.

Add the semolina to the soup, stirring constantly. Let the soup boil for 6 minutes, then add salt to taste. Stir in the heavy cream and serve.

Tomato Soup

2 cups water	Salt
1 heaping tbsp. tomato	4 tbsp. heavy cream
paste	
2 tbsp. finely ground	
semolina	

Bring the water to a boil and stir in the tomato paste.

Add the semolina, stirring constantly. Salt the soup, and let it boil for 6 minutes; then add the heavy cream and serve.

Pumpkin Soup

Take the skin off ½ pound of fresh pumpkin with a
potato peeler. Cut the pulp into pieces the size of a wal-
nut and put them into a pot. Barely cover the pumpkin
with boiling water. Let it boil for 6 to 8 minutes, then
mash up the pumpkin. Add salt and pepper, and a cup
of milk. Bring to a boil and serve. If you like, you can
add a little sugar to the soup before serving.

Aïgo-boulido (Garlic Soup)

2 cloves of garlic
1 bay leaf
1 tbsp. olive oil
2 cups boiling water

Salt and pepper
2 egg yolks
Stale bread, or toast

Crush the garlic by placing it under the flat side of a
knife blade and hitting the blade hard with your fist.
Put the crushed garlic into a pot with the bay leaf and
the olive oil. Pour the boiling water into the pot, add
salt and pepper, and boil the soup for 8 to 10 minutes.
Take the pot off the stove. Place the egg yolks in your
serving bowl, and stir in half a ladle of hot soup. When
the mixture is smooth, add the rest of the soup. Drop 4
small pieces of stale bread, or toast, into the soup and
serve.

If there are two of you, you should both eat this soup.
Because if one of you doesn't, he will be obliged to enjoy the other's company from across the room after
dinner.

Saint-Germain Soup

The only way you will be able to make this soup is by using a vegetable flour (see Introduction, p. xxiv), since split peas take a very long time to cook.

There are many brands of vegetable flour; the best are those which taste the most like the vegetable itself.

Another thing I must tell you is that vegetable flours

don't form a paste when exposed to liquid and heat. So the soup they make doesn't really stay together; the vegetable flour sinks to the bottom of the bowl and the water sits on top. In order to avoid this, add a little ordinary flour to the vegetable flour when making soup. This way, the flour mixes together with the water to form a paste that holds the vegetable flour in suspension.

Now that you know this, let's make Saint-Germain soup:

Place a tablespoon of butter in a saucepan and let it melt. Add a teaspoon of flour, and 2 tablespoons of green-pea flour. Mix everything together over the heat. Little by little, stirring constantly, add 2 cups of warm water and salt. Boil the soup for 6 minutes, drop in a few small pieces of crust from stale bread or toast, and serve.

Esau Soup

Follow the recipe for *Saint-Germain soup*, but replace the green-pea flour with lentil flour.

Fish Soup

1 fish head (hake or cod) or, if unavailable, ½ lb. smelt	1 bay leaf
	1 pinch of saffron
	1 tbsp. olive oil
3 cups boiling water	2 tbsp. rice flour
Salt and pepper	Stale bread, or toast

Cut the head of the hake or codfish into 8 pieces. Place the fish in a pot and cover it with the boiling water.

Add salt, pepper, the bay leaf, the saffron, and the olive oil. While the soup is boiling, put the rice flour into a bowl and dilute it with a little cold water. Pour the contents of the bowl into the soup, stirring constantly; then let it continue boiling for 10 minutes.

Put 6 small pieces of stale bread or toast into a soup tureen; then place a colander over the tureen. Pour the contents of the pot, both soup and fish, into the colander, and mash the fish up with a wooden pestle. Now you can take the tureen with its moistened bread and wonderful bouillon to the table.

EXTEMPORANEOUS SAUCES

Now, you mustn't think that ten-minute cooking condemns you to eating nothing but minute steaks, with none of the refinements of great French cuisine.

Your stove has at least two burners, maybe three. Who can stop you from using one burner to sauté some slices of beef kidney in butter, while you make béarnaise sauce on the other?

In the same ten minutes you can prepare both the

kidneys and the sauce, and the result is absolutely delicious. I've done it many times, and the common beef kidney, scorned by people of delicate taste, takes on a most aristocratic appearance because of the sauce.

So you can always prepare a slice of meat and a sauce. Are there many extemporaneous sauces? That depends on your imagination. Invent them. The main thing is to make them quickly. In order to do that, just follow the basic principles I'm setting down here for making some of the more typical sauces.

White Sauce

This is a horrible sauce. Fortunately, you can add whatever you like to it and transform it into a very nice one.

Technically, white sauce is nothing more than a flour paste with butter and salt in it. This is how you make it:

Take a small saucepan and a wire whisk. Put a generous tablespoon of butter and a scant tablespoon of flour into the pan. As the butter melts over the fire, stir the flour into it with the wire whisk. When the mixture is smooth, add, little by little, ½ cup of cold water, stirring constantly.

As the water becomes hot, the flour turns to paste and the sauce thickens. If any lumps form, squash them immediately. Let the sauce puff up and bubble briefly on the stove, then add salt and take it off the heat. Add a little pat of butter, and when it has melted, stir it into the sauce. Now it's ready. Frankly, it's no good at all, is it? So never use white sauce as it is. Instead, transform it into one of the following sauces.

Normandy Sauce

Make *white sauce* according to the preceding recipe. Take it off the stove and add 4 tablespoons of heavy cream. Mix together well, then put the pot back on the fire. Let it puff up and bubble once; now it's ready.

What should you serve this sauce with? It goes well with boiled fish, for example.

Supreme Sauce

Make *Normandy sauce*. Add a few drops of meat extract to taste. This gives body to the sauce and changes its taste completely.

This sauce is marvelous with fish, *fried veal cutlets,* or any other white meat.

Aurora Sauce

Make *Normandy sauce*. At the last minute add a tiny bit of tomato paste, just enough to color the sauce a beautiful coral pink. If you serve cooked mussels in this sauce, you will receive all kinds of compliments.

Poulette Sauce

Make *white sauce*. Right after you've taken it off the stove, beat into it 2 egg yolks and a few drops of meat extract.

This sauce goes very well with lamb's trotters (feet), which you may be able to find cooked at a tripe dealer's.

In this case, all you have to do is heat up the trotters in the gelatin they come in; this gelatin will turn to bouillon. Heat the lamb's trotters on one burner while you prepare the poulette sauce on another burner. Then drain the trotters and cover them with the sauce.

Béchamel Sauce

This is a *white sauce* which has been considerably improved by the use of milk instead of water to dilute the butter-flour mixture. It is made this way:

Melt a generous tablespoon of butter in a saucepan. Then add a scant tablespoon of flour, mixing the two together with a wire whisk. Stirring constantly, add about ½ cup cold milk. As it mixes together, the sauce will thicken. Bring it to a boil and let it cook until it is the consistency you like. You may want to use more or less milk than indicated. Add salt and a little white pepper, and your sauce is ready. I think you'll agree that it's a great improvement over white sauce. But it can be made better yet.

Mornay Sauce

This is simply a *béchamel sauce* to which you add 2 heaping tablespoons of grated Swiss or Gruyère cheese before serving. Bring the sauce to a boil, stirring constantly after you've added the cheese. Take it off the fire—it's ready. Mornay sauce is good with boiled vegetables. You will have to use reheated, precooked vegetables—they are invaluable in ten-minute cooking.

Curry Sauce

Curry is a mixture of spices prepared in India. The most important ingredients are turmeric and aniseed. There is not just one kind of curry; there are as many curries as there are Indian cooks. Each one buys the different spices that go into curry at the spice market, brings them home, and mixes them in different proportions according to his taste.

Among those prepared commercially, the English curry powders are the best, and contain a typical mixture of spices.

To make French-style curry sauce, first make a *béchamel sauce*. Then, according to your taste, add as much curry powder as you want. For the proportions I've given, you will need at least ½ teaspoon of curry powder.

Mix the curry powder in well, bring the sauce back to a boil, and serve over *hard-boiled eggs, five-minute eggs,* or whatever you like.

Piquant Sauce

1 tbsp. butter
½ onion, chopped fine
1 tbsp. flour
½ cup cold water

1 tsp. wine vinegar
3 small vinegar pickles
Meat extract

Up until now, we have been making only white sauces. Brown sauces also have a butter-flour base, but it is allowed to cook until it turns brown before liquid is added. This is what cooks call a "roux."

The roux will take less time to make if you brown a little onion in the butter before adding the flour. Piquant sauce is a brown sauce. Prepare it as follows:

Put a frying pan on the fire, place a tablespoon of butter in it and wait until the butter begins to smoke. Now add the onion. Turn up the heat, and stir the onion around in the butter. It will color rapidly, first turning gold, then reddish, then mahogany brown. When it reaches this last stage, add the flour, mix together well, and as soon as the flour browns, add the cold water, stirring the sauce constantly with a wire whisk. Bring the sauce to a boil, add the vinegar, and bring back to a boil. Now add the pickles sliced into circles, and a little meat extract. This sauce is perfect. It can be used to accompany pork chops cooked in a frying pan on the other burner.

Mustard Sauce

Make a *piquant sauce*, but instead of adding pickles, add a teaspoon of hot Dijon mustard. This sauce is often served with fried herring.

Sauce Robert

Make a *mustard sauce*. At the last minute, add 2 teaspoons tomato paste. This sauce is excellent on either veal or pork.

Mayonnaise

Will you ever have the opportunity to eat mayonnaise? Of course. Homemade mayonnaise gives a personal touch to the slice of cold roast beef or other meat that your butcher has prepared. Ordinary things take on a special distinction when served with homemade mayonnaise. Nothing is easier to make.

You need a fresh egg and a bottle of salad oil. Both should be at room temperature. This is especially true of the oil. If it is too cold, it will be partly solidified and your mayonnaise will be a total failure.

Break the egg and place the yolk in a bowl. If there are two of you, have the other person pour the oil. You will be armed with a wire whisk, or simply a fork, with which you will stir the egg-yolk-and-oil mixture. Your partner will pour the oil *very slowly*; a few drops at a time in the beginning, then in a very thin dribble as the sauce thickens. This won't take long. When it is the

right consistency, add salt and a few drops of vinegar.
Serve it with fish or cold meat.

Hollandaise Sauce

Many people, including some good cooks, think that hollandaise sauce is very difficult to make. Actually, I can't
think of anything easier. If you do just as I say, you will
certainly succeed.

Put a teaspoon of water, a little salt, and 2 egg yolks
into a small saucepan. If you like lemon, add a few drops
of lemon juice. It will both improve the flavor and in-
crease your chances of making a perfect hollandaise
sauce.

Place the saucepan in a larger pot containing boiling
water, but don't let go of the saucepan. With a wire
whisk or a fork, quickly mix the egg yolks with the other
ingredients, stirring constantly. The mixture will soon
begin to thicken. Take the saucepan immediately out of

the water, and add to its contents 4 tablespoons of butter. Put the saucepan back into the hot water, stirring
constantly with the whisk. The pieces of butter will
melt, and the sauce will become creamy. Lift the pot out
of the water again and add 4 more tablespoons of
butter; stir, and put the saucepan back into the water,
stirring all the while. As the sauce begins to thicken, stick
your finger into it now and again. When you feel a burning sensation, take the pot out of the water and stir
quickly for another fifteen seconds or so. Your sauce is
ready. It should be rich and creamy enough to coat a
spoon, but not as thick as mayonnaise.

If you follow my instructions carefully, you will find
that, like me, you will never make a hollandaise sauce
that isn't perfect. So don't be afraid of it. It's delicious
with boiled fish or canned asparagus that have been
heated up in their juice.

Béarnaise Sauce

1 shallot, finely chopped	Salt
2 tbsp. wine vinegar	2 egg yolks
1 tbsp. cold water	A ¼ lb. stick of butter

Béarnaise sauce is actually *hollandaise sauce* flavored
with shallot and vinegar.

Peel a shallot and chop it up as fine as possible. Place
it in a saucepan with the vinegar. Put the pot on the
burner and let the contents boil until the vinegar has
evaporated almost completely. Now add a tablespoon of
cold water and a little salt. Take the pot off the stove and

add the egg yolks; then proceed as you would for hollandaise sauce—that is, place the saucepan in a pot of boiling water when adding the butter. Béarnaise sauce is a refined accompaniment to a minute steak or any broiled meat.

Tomato Sauce

Melt a tablespoon of butter in a small saucepan, add a tablespoon of tomato paste, and mix the two together well. Little by little, add hot water, stirring constantly, to dilute the sauce. Stop when it is the consistency you like and add salt.

SOME QUICKLY PREPARED EGG DISHES

Soft-Boiled Eggs

Nothing is easier than cooking soft-boiled eggs. You have a pot of boiling water on the stove. Take 2 fresh eggs, place them one by one on a spoon, and lower them delicately into the boiling water. If there is enough water in the pot, it should come back to a boil immediately. Wait 2½ minutes, take the eggs out of the water, put them into egg cups, and, without waiting a second longer, slice the top of the shell off with a knife. Eat the

eggs sprinkled with salt, accompanied by buttered toast and a dry white wine. They're delicious.

Five-Minute Eggs

Cook 2 fresh eggs for 5 minutes in boiling water. Then take them out of the pot and put them into a bowl of cold water. Leave them there for 10 seconds. Now peel them very carefully without breaking the whites of the eggs. Place the eggs on a plate and serve them with melted butter, *mornay sauce,* or *tomato sauce.*

Hard-Boiled Eggs

Cook 2 eggs as you would *five-minute eggs,* but boil them for 10 minutes. When they're done, take them out of the pot and put them into a bowl of cold water. Leave them there until they have cooled off.

Serve with salt, butter, and hot Dijon mustard. They're even better with a little grated horseradish that has been lightly seasoned with vinegar.

Hard-boiled eggs are complemented by any cold sauce, such as *mayonnaise,* oil-and-vinegar dressing, or *tomato sauce.*

Poached Eggs

Poached eggs are very easy to make. Fill a medium-size saucepan half full with boiling water—it's there on the stove. Break a very fresh egg into a teacup. Tip the cup, holding it very close to the surface of the boiling water, so that the egg slips gently into the pot. The white will coagulate immediately, and the egg will take a more or less symmetrical oblong shape. Let it boil a full minute, then lift it out of the water with a skimmer. Let the water drain off, then place the egg on a plate and cut off any irregular pieces of egg white. Cook the second egg as you did the first. Pour over them melted butter, brown butter, one of the white sauces, or a brown sauce made with red Burgundy wine instead of water. This last combination is called poached eggs meurette.

French-Fried Eggs

Fill a pot halfway with cooking oil and place it on the stove. Break an egg into a teacup, and when the oil is hot (that is, when it begins to smoke), drop the egg into it.

The egg white will puff up at once and form big bubbles. Pierce them with a fork and wait 30 or 40 seconds.

Take the egg out of the oil with a skimmer. Place it on a warm platter and salt it. Cook the second immediately after the first.

Eggs cooked in this way are an excellent accompaniment to breakfast sausages which have been fried in butter for 6 to 7 minutes.

Eggs "Sur le Plat"

Take a shallow fireproof dish made of porcelain or metal and put it on the burner. Place a tablespoon of butter in it, and when the butter has melted, break 2 eggs into the dish, making sure not to hold them up too high when you let them fall. The white will coagulate immediately. Pierce it here and there so it will cook evenly on the top and bottom, but don't touch the yolk whatever you do. When the white is cooked, put the dish on a plate and serve. Sprinkle the eggs with salt, and eat them by dipping pieces of toast first in the yolk, then in the white, then in the butter. Not very elegant, but absolutely delicious.

Eggs and Bacon

For this dish, use only the highest quality bacon. It should be very lean, and well cured—a superior product. It will be expensive, but it won't ruin you.

Melt a tablespoon of butter in a fireproof dish, then lower the heat. Take 2 slices of bacon, cut each one in half, and place the pieces so that they cover the bottom of the dish. Wait until the fat melts and becomes transparent. Then break 2 eggs into the dish, raise the heat, and finish cooking them according to the instructions given for making *eggs "sur le plat."* Salt and pepper very lightly. Place the dish on a plate and serve, adding a dash of Worcestershire sauce if you like.

Ham and Eggs

Buy a slice of cooked ham, Virginia ham if possible. Then follow the recipe for *eggs and bacon*, replacing the bacon with the ham.

Eggs and Cervelat

Buy a cervelat (saveloy sausage). Take off the skin and cut it into ¼-inch slices. Follow the recipe for *eggs and bacon*, replacing the bacon with 3 slices of saveloy sausage.

This recipe will use only about half your sausage. The rest can be an hors d'oeuvre, cut into cubes and seasoned with salad oil, vinegar, and mustard.

Eggs with Cream

Heat a tablespoon of butter in a fireproof dish. Break 2 eggs into the dish, and proceed as you would for *eggs "sur le plat."* When the eggs are half cooked, add 2 teaspoons heavy cream, spreading it around the dish. Season the eggs with salt and paprika, and serve them hot, with a nice cold glass of white wine.

Scrambled Eggs

It takes two to scramble. That's why you always make scrambled eggs, not scrambled egg. One really doesn't work, since it cooks much too fast.

Break 2 eggs into a bowl, beat them up with a fork, and add a little salt.

Place a generous tablespoon of butter into a frying pan and wait until it gets good and hot. Then pour in the eggs and let them cook just a little. Now take a fork and scrape the cooked part off the bottom of the pan, mixing it in with the rest. Lower the flame and beat the eggs until they are of a creamy consistency; then remove the pan from the fire. Keep stirring them, since they will continue to cook even though they are off the stove. When they are ready, that is, cooked but still creamy, slide them onto a warm plate and eat them immediately.

You can add all sorts of things to the scrambled eggs before they've finished cooking. For example:

Saveloy sausage cut into cubes
Diced ham
Canned peas
Peeled shrimp
Cooked mussels
Little pieces of bread fried in butter
Mushrooms sautéed in butter
Bits of truffle
Etc. . . .

But don't forget that these various elements should be added only in very small quantities. Scrambled eggs with green peas shouldn't be green peas with scrambled eggs. The main thing you should taste is the creamy eggs. The garnish should always be a secondary taste.

For that matter, eggs with little green peas are very pretty, whereas green peas with eggs look pathetic.

Omelet

Making a good omelet is the simplest thing in the world. Success depends a great deal on your frying pan, which must have an absolutely flat bottom; omelets will stick to a warped pan.

Break 2 eggs into a bowl, beat them well, and salt them. Place a generous tablespoon of butter into a frying pan, and as soon as it smokes, add the eggs. The eggs will coagulate as soon as they hit the hot pan, so shake the pan back and forth to prevent them from sticking to it. Then, with a fork, lift the edges of the omelet, tipping the pan toward the fork so that the uncooked egg will slide under the cooked egg. Shake the pan some more.

When the omelet is cooked on the bottom, but creamy and just the slightest bit liquid on top, get a serving platter ready. Tip the pan until the omelet slides and touches the platter, then turn the frying pan upside down, as if you were trying to cover the platter with it. This will make the omelet roll over on top of itself. There it is in the middle of the platter. Serve it immediately.

One of the secrets to making a perfect omelet is never to use too many eggs for the frying pan you have. So don't try to make a six-egg omelet in a pan that won't hold more than two or three.

Like scrambled eggs, omelets can be varied by adding different garnishes to them. For some ideas, consult the list I gave under *scrambled eggs*.

SOME TEN-MINUTE NOODLE DISHES

In France, macaroni, spaghetti, lasagna, and noodles are always overcooked and served in a formless mass. That's why they are not very popular here. So let's cook some noodles right.

To prevent their sticking together, noodles have to be cooked in a large quantity of boiling salted water. Now you will bless that big pot of water you put on the stove when you first walked into the kitchen.

As soon as the noodles are in the water, turn up the heat as high as possible; the water will come back to a boil, but be careful it doesn't boil over. Lower the heat a little and wait. In about 8 to 10 minutes the noodles will be cooked. They are ready when they no longer crunch under your teeth. Now you can do lots of things with them.

Noodles English Style

Cook the noodles in boiling salted water as described above. When they are done, empty the pot into a colander. Let the water drain off the noodles, then put them back into the pot with a large lump of butter. When the butter has melted, mix it with the noodles and serve.

A quarter of a pound of noodles is enough for two people.

Noodles Italian Style

Make some *noodles English style*. Add some tomato paste to them while they're in the pot with the butter, then serve. At the table, sprinkle a little grated Parmesan cheese over them.

Noodles Czechoslovakian Style

Make some *noodles English style*. Before serving, add chopped ham to taste and mix it in with the noodles. Serve as is, without cheese.

Noodles Spanish Style

Make some *noodles English style*. Before serving, add some cooked mussels to them.

Noodles with Gravy

Cook some noodles in boiling salted water. Prepare *fried veal scallops* on another burner while the noodles are cooking. When ready to serve, put the scallops on a platter and pour a little hot water into the frying pan to

dissolve the meat glaze. This will make a light gravy. Drain the noodles, mix them with the gravy, and serve them with the fried veal scallops.

Alsatian Dumplings

Beat an egg with ⅓ cup milk in a bowl. Little by little, add flour, mixing it in with a wire whisk until you have a smooth, thick batter that has a firm consistency. Break any lumps that may have formed.

You already have a pot of salted water on the stove. It's boiling now.

Take a spoonful of batter, dip it into the boiling water for a fraction of a second, then give the spoon a whack on the edge of the pot. The ball of batter will fall into the water.

Work quickly, using up all the batter; there should be at least 15 little dumplings. Let them boil for 5 minutes, making sure the water doesn't boil over; then pour them into a colander and let the water drain off.

Put the dumplings back into the pot, without any water, and add a nice lump of butter. When the butter has completely melted, serve the dumplings. They can be seasoned in a variety of ways: with *tomato sauce,* meat gravy, little pieces of fried bacon, sour cream, butter and grated cheese, etc. There are as many dumpling dishes as there are sauces and garnishes.

Ravioli

In Italian specialty stores you can buy fresh, uncooked ravioli. Their preparation is up to you. Just drop them into a pot of boiling salted water and cook them for 8 to 10 minutes. Drain them, pour some *tomato sauce* over them, sprinkle them with grated Parmesan cheese, and serve.

FISH: FROM THE FRYING PAN ONTO YOUR PLATE

Ten minutes is just enough time to boil a small fish, but it's more than enough time to pan-fry one. Deep frying is even quicker. So you can vary your menus considerably, and not just on Friday, by replacing meat dishes with fish.

Whiting Boiled in Court Bouillon

Salt	Curry powder
1 tbsp. vinegar	1 whiting, cleaned
1 bay leaf	Butter
Pepper	Lemon juice
Nutmeg	Bread crumbs

Salt your boiling pot of water and add the vinegar, a bay leaf, and a few spices such as pepper, nutmeg, curry, etc. Wash the whiting off, then drop it into this court bouillon and let it boil for 10 minutes. While it is cooking, melt a lump of butter in a saucepan and add a little lemon juice to it.

When the fish is cooked, take it out of the water very carefully so it won't break. Place on a platter, pour the melted lemon butter over it, and sprinkle with bread crumbs; then serve.

Skate with Black Butter

Cook 1 pound of skate for 10 minutes in a pot of boiling water seasoned with salt and vinegar.

While the skate is cooking, melt 4 tablespoons butter in a frying pan. Add some fresh chopped parsley to it. The parsley will brown, and the butter will too—first light brown, then mahogany. *Take it off the fire. Wait a few minutes.* Now add a teaspoon of vinegar. The butter shouldn't foam too much, because it has already cooled off a little. If you hadn't waited, it would have splattered all over the place as soon as the cold vinegar touched it.

Take the skate out of the water and drain it well. Place on a platter, pour the black butter over it, add pepper and a little salt if needed; then serve.

Smoked Haddock English Style

Wash ½ pound smoked haddock in cold water. Place it in a pot of boiling, unsalted water and cook 10 minutes. Remove it from the water and let it drain well. Serve with melted butter and lemon juice.

Hake with Tomato Sauce

Bring to a boil a pot of salted water, highly seasoned with fresh herbs and spices. Drop into it 2 slices of hake (or cod), about 1 inch thick each. Let them boil for 10 minutes, then drain and serve with *tomato sauce*.

Anglerfish with Mornay Sauce

Cook a ½-pound piece of anglerfish (or halibut) for 10 minutes in boiling, salted water which has been highly seasoned with fresh herbs and spices. Drain the fish and serve it with *mornay sauce*.

Any fish can be cooked in highly seasoned salted water in 10 minutes, provided it is cut into slices no more than an inch thick. By serving different fish with different sauces, you can vary your meals as much as you like.

Fried Herring

Put some cooking oil into a frying pan and place it on the stove. Take a cleaned fresh herring, wipe it off, and roll it in flour. When the oil starts to smoke, place the fish in the frying pan, lower the flame, and . . . open the window, because it will smell pretty strong. Let the herring brown on one side for 5 minutes, turn it over, let it cook 5 minutes longer, and it's ready. Sprinkle it with salt and serve as is, or with its classical accompaniment—*mustard sauce*.

Fried Mackerel

Have your fish seller clean a mackerel. Wash it and wipe it off when you get home. Make 2 or 3 slits in each side with a knife, and roll the fish in flour. Cook it for 10 minutes in a frying pan containing smoking hot oil or very hot butter. Sprinkle the mackerel with salt and chopped parsley before serving.

I forgot to tell you to open the window. I'll bet you did, anyway.

Fresh Sardines

Take some fresh sardines and gut them. To do this, cut just through the backbone behind the head. Pull the head off; the intestines will be pulled out at the same time.

Once this is done, rinse the fish off, wipe each one with a dry towel, then fry them in a little smoking oil or very hot butter. There's no need to roll them in flour.

Cook them very quickly over a hot burner. Don't salt them, just serve them as they are with a curl of fresh butter and half a lemon.

Trout Meunière

This dish is considered a luxury. Unfortunately, in large cities it doesn't bring the satisfaction the price of these precious fish would seem to suggest. The reason for this is that, in cities, the trout you get are "artificial." They are born and raised on fish farms and fed too scientifically. The result is a flabby fish which bears almost no resemblance to the trout that live in mountain streams.

They should be prepared like herring, that is, cleaned,

washed, wiped dry, rolled in flour, and fried in butter that is very hot but not brown. When the fish is cooked, salt it and serve it with the butter it cooked in. It's a good idea to add fresh butter to the cooked butter before you pour it over the trout.

Trout au Bleu

Put a cup of vinegar into a saucepan and bring it to a boil. At the same time, heat a pot full of salted water which has been highly seasoned with fresh herbs and spices—a court bouillon.

For this recipe you should use live trout. Kill them by whacking the top of their heads against the edge of a table. Clean and wash them, then wipe them off. Place them in a deep platter and pour the *boiling* vinegar over them. They will turn sky-blue. Now place them immediately into the boiling court bouillon and cook them for 7 to 8 minutes. Remove them from the pot, drain them, and serve with melted butter.

Filets of Sole with Mushrooms

¼ lb. fresh mushrooms	Salt and pepper
Butter	¼ cup white wine
4 filets of sole	Flour

Cut the sandy part off the mushroom stems, and wash the mushrooms in a large basin of water. Throw the water away, along with the sand that has fallen into it. Wash the mushrooms a second time. Don't bother to peel them; that's only a waste of time. Cut them into slices, wash them one last time, drain them, and pat them dry with a towel.

Place a generous tablespoon of butter in a frying pan. When it begins to smoke, add the sole, brown them for 1 minute, then turn them over and brown them for 1 minute on the other side. Add the mushrooms (they'll give out water), and sprinkle with salt and pepper. Add the wine, and bring to a furious boil. The water will evaporate. All this has taken 10 minutes. Now lower the heat and add a lump of soft butter which has been mixed with a little flour until it is smooth and creamy. Stir it into the sauce as it melts, then pour everything onto a platter and serve.

When you turn the heat down for the last step, there should be just enough liquid in the pan to make a nice sauce. So as you're boiling the water off, regulate the heat to keep the sauce from evaporating too much.

Flounder Meunière

Wash a flounder that has already been gutted. Wipe it off and roll it in flour. Fry it in smoking hot butter, and when it is done, sprinkle it with salt. Serve with a slice of lemon.

Deep-Fried Smelt

When you walk in the door, put a pot half filled with cooking oil on the stove.

Clean some smelt, wipe them off, and roll them in

flour. Drop them into the smoking oil. Let them cook for 3 minutes, then take them out. Reheat the oil for 3 minutes, then drop the fish into it again, this time for 2 minutes. Take them out of the pot, drain them, and sprinkle them with salt. Serve with slices of lemon.

Deep-Fried Whiting

Whiting have to be small for deep frying, otherwise they won't be cooked in 10 minutes.

Wash 2 small whiting which have already been gutted. Wipe them off and roll them in flour. Then cook them and serve according to the recipe for *deep-fried smelt*.

Sliced Hake Viennese Style

2 slices hake, each ¾″ thick	Bread crumbs
Cooking oil	Salt
Flour	Slices of lemon
1 egg, beaten	2 sprigs of parsley

Put a pot half full of oil on the stove. While it's heating, take 3 plates. Put some flour into the first, the egg into the second, and bread crumbs into the third.

Dip your fish slices (1) into the flour, (2) into the egg, (3) into the bread crumbs. Then drop them into the hot oil, which should be really smoking. In 8 minutes they will be ready. To serve, sprinkle the fish with salt and decorate them with slices of lemon and the sprigs of parsley, which have been cooked for 20 seconds in the deep fat.

Salt Cod English Style

Buy a package of salt cod. It's very practical because it keeps a long time, so you can use as much or as little as you want. One filet will be enough for one person, so take it out of the package and put the rest away in a dry place for the next time.

If you plan on having salt cod for lunch one day, you have to soak it in cold water the night before. Change the water two or three times. At lunchtime, drop the desalted filet of cod into a pot of boiling, unsalted water. Let it cook for 5 to 6 minutes, drain, and put on a platter. Pour some melted butter over it and serve with a slice of lemon. Drink a glass of dry white wine with it—or two glasses, because they say that codfish has a thirst for butter and gives a thirst to anyone who eats it.

Creamed Salt Cod

Cook the cod according to the preceding recipe. While it is cooking, make *Normandy sauce*. Mix the fish and the sauce together and savor it.

Salt Cod Biscaïenne

Cook the cod according to the recipe for *salt cod English style*. While it is cooking, follow the recipe for *tomato sauce*, but replace the butter in that recipe with olive oil. Cut a green pepper into thin slices and add it to the sauce. Let it cook for 5 to 6 minutes; then pour the sauce over the cod and serve.

The traditional way of serving this dish is to cut a large green pepper in half lengthwise, remove the seeds, place a piece of cooked codfish in each of the pepper halves, and pour the sauce over them. It's possible to do all this in ten—well, twelve—minutes.

Deep-Fried Salt Cod

Put a pot half full of cooking oil on the burner. Take a filet of salt cod which has been desalted. Cut it into strips and roll the strips in flour, then drop them into the smoking hot oil. Cook them for 8 to 10 minutes, then serve with some sprigs of fresh parsley which have been deep fried as well.

Sautéed Frogs' Legs

12 frogs' legs	4 tbsp. butter
Flour	Lemon
1 egg, beaten	Fresh parsley
Bread crumbs	

The frog isn't a fish, but since they're neighbors, we'll put them in the same chapter.

Buy a dozen frogs' legs. Get 3 plates ready. Put flour into the first, the egg into the second, and some bread crumbs into the third. Put the butter into a frying pan and heat until it nearly smokes.

Meanwhile, roll the frogs' legs in (1) the flour, (2) the egg, (3) the bread crumbs. Press the bread crumbs into the frogs' legs with your fingers.

Cook the frogs' legs in the hot butter; 5 minutes is long enough. Serve with lemon and some chopped parsley.

Frogs' Legs Poulette

Sauté 12 frogs' legs in butter. While they are cooking, make *poulette sauce*. Mix the frogs' legs and sauce together and serve, sprinkled lightly with finely chopped parsley.

SHELLFISH,
LOBSTERS & CO.

SHELLFISH

The number of shellfish that can be prepared in ten minutes is relatively limited. We mustn't forget them, though, because they can make elegant entrées and are very nourishing.

The easiest preparation consists of fresh oysters which have been opened for you at the fish market. Bring them home and eat them seasoned with a few drops of lemon juice. Accompany them with thin slices of brown bread

and lots of butter, and drink an ice-cold, dry white wine.

Oysters and Sausages

This dish is a favorite in Bordeaux.

Fry some small link sausages. Serve them very hot on one platter, and on a second platter serve a dozen freshly opened oysters.

Alternate sensations: burn your mouth with a hot, crunchy sausage, then soothe your burns with a cool, smooth oyster. Continue in this way until you have finished off both the sausages and the oysters.

Cold white wine, of course.

Snails in Their Shells

Buy a dozen snails, already prepared with garlic butter, from a trustworthy merchant—that is, someone who uses only the best butter for his snails.

Arrange the snails in a shallow baking dish. This isn't as easy as it might seem, since the opening of the snail shell should be facing up. Otherwise all the butter will run out when it melts and the snail will be dried out and tough.

Now that the snails are arranged, put a tiny bit of water into the baking dish, and put the dish on the burner for 2 or 3 minutes, just long enough to heat it. Then place the dish under the broiler for 5 to 6 minutes. By then the butter will have melted and the snails will be hot. Serve them immediately, while they're still hot enough to burn your fingers.

Mussels Marinière

Take 2 pounds of mussels whose shells have already been scraped clean. Wash them in cold running water, making sure that each mussel is good. To do this, try to slide one shell sideways against the other. If the shells slide easily and the mussel opens, it's no good. Just throw it away. It will undoubtedly contain silt, which would completely pollute your dinner. This silt is not only dirty, it smells awful.

Once the mussels are washed, put them in a pot without water and cover them. Place them on a hot burner; in about 5 minutes all the shells will have opened and the water they contained will have started to boil. The mussels are cooked.

Add a little pepper, some finely chopped parsley, and 4 tablespoons of butter, which will melt in the mussel water.

This dish is as exquisite as it is simple.

Mussels Poulette

If you want to make a dish worthy of a great French chef, cook your mussels according to the preceding recipe. When they're cooked, leave them in their shells and place them in a serving dish. Strain the mussel water into a small saucepan. Add some butter and heat the sauce. Then take it off the heat and stir in 1 or 2 egg yolks—make sure the sauce isn't boiling when you do this. Serve the sauce in a sauceboat.

Mussels with Saffron

2 lb. (1 qt.) fresh mussels	1 tsp. flour
2 tbsp. butter	⅓ cup heavy cream
Saffron	

Cook the mussels according to the recipe for *mussels marinière*. Remove them from the liquid they produced while cooking. Strain then heat this mussel water with the butter and a little saffron. Mix the flour and the heavy cream, and stir this mixture into the sauce. Serve the mussels in a soup plate, and the sauce in a sauceboat. This dish is a real treat.

L O B S T E R S   &   C O .

Cooked shrimp can be eaten just as they are. Canned lobster is good decorated with a little mayonnaise. These are the first things that come to mind when thinking of the lobster family, but a few other ten-minute dishes can be prepared as well.

Hot Boiled Shrimp

Live shrimp are sold in some cities. Wash ¼ pound of them while you're waiting for a small pot of water to come to a boil on the stove.

Salt the water heavily, and when it boils, drop in the shrimp—don't let them jump out of the pot. Cook for 5 minutes and serve them very hot with freshly buttered bread.

Scampi American Style

1 tbsp. olive oil	½ lb. scampi
1 generous tbsp. tomato paste	Paprika or cayenne pepper
Salt	1 tbsp. cognac
½ cup white wine	Fresh parsley
¼ cup Madeira	

Heat the olive oil in a pot. Add the tomato paste and salt lightly. Thin the mixture with the wine and Madeira. Now add the scampi and season with paprika or a *hint* of cayenne pepper. Cover and cook for 8 minutes, then add the cognac. Cook for 2 more minutes; then add more salt if it needs it. Sprinkle with chopped parsley, sit down, and enjoy yourself.

Lobster with Mayonnaise

Buy half a cooked lobster. Serve it with homemade *mayonnaise*. That won't take very long to make, so spend the extra time decorating the serving platter with a few lettuce leaves, some black and green olives, capers, or anything else that comes to mind. You will feel yourself becoming an artist.

SOME VEGETABLES
AND GARNISHES

I have decided to talk about vegetables before I pass on to the meat dishes. But, you may say, that's going against habit and tradition. That's right, but we mustn't forget that we are upsetting tradition entirely by making vegetable dishes in ten minutes, even though a half hour is usually required just to cook the vegetables before preparing the dish itself.

So this section will be reduced to covering only those vegetables which cook in a few minutes—vegetable flours and canned vegetables almost exclusively. (See Introduction, p. xxiv). In preparing the following vegetable dishes, which will be used mainly to garnish pan-fried meats, we are really just reheating what has already been cooked.

POTATOES

It is a good idea to keep potatoes which have been boiled and left in their skins on hand for ten-minute cooking. A number of dishes can be prepared with them.

Boiled Potatoes

Take some cooked potatoes with their skins on. Drop
them into a pot of boiling water and cook them for 5 to
8 minutes, depending on how big they are.

Serve wrapped in a napkin, with curls of fresh butter.

Sautéed Potatoes

Peel some cooked, cold potatoes, and cut into slices a
good ¼ inch thick.

Heat a lump of butter and a tablespoon of oil in a frying pan until they begin to smoke. Drop in the potatoes,
and shake the pan to keep them from sticking to the
bottom. Brown for 3 minutes, then turn over. Cook 6
minutes more over high heat, salt, and serve with a
steak or veal cutlet.

Potato Salad

Slice some cooked potatoes as you would for *sautéed
potatoes*. Mix them in a salad bowl with oil, vinegar, a
teaspoon of cold water, salt, pepper, and, when in season,
some freshly chopped tarragon.

Potatoes and Bacon

Cut some cooked potatoes into thin slices.

Heat a small lump of butter in a frying pan, then add
2 slices of bacon, cut into little pieces.

When the fat on the bacon has melted, sauté the potatoes in it, sprinkle lightly with salt, and serve.

Stewed Potatoes

Cooked potatoes
Butter
1 onion, finely chopped
2 tsp. flour

Cold water
Salt and pepper
½ bay leaf

Peel the potatoes, and cut them into slices an inch thick.

Melt a lump of butter in a frying pan, and add the onion. When the onion is nice and brown, add the flour. Brown the flour, then add cold water little by little, until the boiling sauce is the consistency of gravy. Add salt, pepper, the bay leaf, and the potatoes. Heat for 5 minutes and serve.

Potatoes Béchamel

Cut some cooked potatoes into thin slices. Make some *béchamel sauce* and mix it with the potatoes. Reheat the mixture very carefully, because it will stick to the pan. If you like, you can add a little grated Swiss cheese and call your dish Potatoes Mornay.

French-Fried Potatoes

Place a pot half full of cooking oil on the stove. Peel some raw potatoes and cut into slices ⅛ inch thick. When the oil starts to smoke, drop the potatoes into the pot. Let them cook for 5 minutes, then take them out and heat the fat until it begins to smoke again. Put the potatoes back into the pot for 2 minutes more, then take them out, drain them, and salt them lightly.

P E A S

A small can of peas is enough for two or three people. Open the can and separate the peas from their juice; there's always too much of it. Keep the juice for use in the following recipes.

Buttered Green Peas

Melt a lump of butter in a saucepan. Add to it the peas and 2 tablespoons of their juice. Let them boil for 5 minutes. If there's not enough liquid, add a little more, but don't add so much that the peas swim in it. After all, you're not making pea soup.

Green Peas with Bacon

Melt a small lump of butter in a saucepan and add 2 slices of bacon cut up into very small pieces. When the fat on the bacon has melted, add the peas and 2 or 3 tablespoons of their juice. Bring to a boil and cook for 5 to 6 minutes; then serve.

Green Peas with Ham

Follow the recipe for *buttered green peas*. Halfway through the cooking time, add a slice of ham that has been cut into thin strips, and cook until the peas are done.

Green Peas with Cream

Follow the recipe for *buttered green peas*. While the peas are heating up, mix 4 tablespoons heavy cream with ½ teaspoon flour. When this mixture is smooth, add it to the peas and bring just to a boil. If the sauce is too thick, add some of the juice the peas came in. Sprinkle with salt, but don't add any pepper, and serve.

GREEN BEANS

Canned green beans are already cooked, of course. All you have to do is heat them up in their juice.

Green Beans Maître d'Hôtel

Open a can of green beans and pour the contents into a pot. Bring to a boil and then simmer for 5 minutes or less. Drain the beans in a colander and throw away their juice.

Put the beans back into the pot, on the stove. Add 4 tablespoons butter and mix with the beans, stirring delicately so that the beans don't fall apart. When the butter has melted, add some chopped parsley, salt lightly if needed, and serve.

Green Beans with Sour Cream

Follow the recipe for *green beans maître d'hôtel.* Just before serving, add 2 generous tablespoons sour cream. Mix well but gently, and serve when hot. This is an attractive dish.

Sautéed Green Beans

Open a can of green beans and pour the contents into a colander. Let the beans drain.

Put 3 tablespoons butter into a frying pan, and when it begins to smoke, add the beans. They will begin to fry in the butter. Stir them around, turning them over several times. Salt, pepper lightly, and serve.

Green Bean Salad

Drain a can of green beans in a colander. Serve them

seasoned with salad oil, vinegar, salt, pepper, and finely chopped fresh herbs. This is a good summer dish.

WHITE KIDNEY BEANS AND BABY LIMAS

Both white kidney beans and baby limas can be bought already cooked in cans. The contents of the can are simply heated up and seasoned according to taste.

White Kidney Beans Breton Style

Drain a can of white kidney beans in a strainer—save the juice. Melt 4 tablespoons of butter in a saucepan, then add the beans and 2 to 3 tablespoons of their juice.

Heat for 5 minutes, adding a little more juice if necessary. Sprinkle with salt and decorate with some chopped parsley before serving.

Sautéed White Kidney Beans

Heat 4 tablespoons butter in a frying pan until it smokes. Add a drained can of white kidney beans. Let them brown a little—they're ready.

The best way to sauté white kidney beans is to cook them with a pork chop or a veal cutlet. They should be added a couple of minutes before the meat is done— just long enough for them to heat up thoroughly. Cooked in this way, they have a nice meaty flavor, which makes them even better.

White Kidney Beans Basque Style

Heat 2 tablespoons olive oil in a frying pan. Add ½ clove of garlic, chopped up fine. When the garlic begins to brown, add a drained can of white kidney beans, stir, then add just a little of their juice. Add salt and lots of pepper, and serve hot.

Baby Limas in Cream Sauce

2½ tbsp. butter	½ tsp. flour
1 can baby limas	Fresh parsley, chopped
2 tbsp. sour cream	

Melt the butter in a saucepan. Add the lima beans, and 3 tablespoons of their juice.

Mix the sour cream with the flour in a bowl. When smooth, add the cream mixture to the beans and bring just to a boil. Serve immediately, sprinkled with parsley.

S A U E R K R A U T

Buy some cooked sauerkraut, either in a can or at the local delicatessen. You will never have time to cook it yourself.

Really excellent sauerkraut is cooked with goose or chicken fat, and if little scraps of meat have been added, so much the better.

Sauerkraut Alsatian Style

1 tbsp. white Alsatian wine (if unavailable use a German white wine)
Cooked sauerkraut
Strasbourg sausages (if unavailable use frankfurter sausages)

1 slice ham
Hot Dijon mustard

Add a tablespoon of white Alsatian wine to the sauerkraut and heat it up in a pot. Meanwhile, boil some Strasbourg sausages in water for 5 minutes.

When done, serve the sauerkraut garnished with the sausages and a slice of ham. Don't forget to put hot Dijon mustard on the table when you serve this dish.

Sauerkraut with Flat Sausages

Heat up the sauerkraut. On another burner, fry some round, flat sausages. When they're nice and brown, serve with the sauerkraut.

Sauerkraut Salad

Buy ½ pound uncooked sauerkraut at the local delicatessen. Wash it 3 times in cold running water so that it won't be too acid. Press it dry in a towel, then season it with salad oil and salt.

This salad is an excellent accompaniment to fried breakfast sausages.

A R T I C H O K E S

Take 2 boiled artichokes. Serve them with an oil-and-vinegar dressing, highly seasoned with hot Dijon mustard.

A S P A R A G U S

Ten minutes isn't long enough to cook fresh asparagus, so you will have to buy it canned. (The best is usually sold in glass jars.) Although much softer than freshly boiled asparagus, the precooked variety is tasty, nevertheless.

Asparagus Salad

Serve some canned asparagus cold, with a dressing made of salad oil, vinegar, salt, and pepper.

Asparagus with Hollandaise Sauce

Heat some canned asparagus in their juice. At the same time, make *hollandaise sauce*. Serve the asparagus on a platter, the sauce in a bowl.

P U M P K I N

Buy a pound of fresh pumpkin. Cut off all the skin; don't worry about wasting anything, as it's better to take off too much than too little.

Cut the pulp into ½-inch squares. Melt some butter in a frying pan, then add the pumpkin. When it has softened, which it will do very quickly, add lots of salt and pepper.

If you prefer, you can add sugar to the pumpkin instead of salt and pepper, and serve it for dessert.

B E E T S

The beet is an excellent vegetable. Unfortunately, it is not fully appreciated, at least not in France. You can buy precooked beets or cook them yourself and store them for later use in ten-minute cooking.

Chopped Beets in Cream Sauce

Peel and rinse ½ pound cooked beets, then wipe them off and chop them up fine. Melt some butter in a frying pan, and when it begins to smoke, add the beets. When they're hot, add salt and a teaspoon of wine vinegar. The beets will immediately turn bright red. Add 4 tablespoons heavy cream, mix it in with the beets, and cook 2 minutes longer. Serve them with a pork chop or *quail en cocotte*.

Beet Salad with Sour Cream

Cut the beets into slices and season them with vinegar and salt. Then place them in a dish and cover them with sour cream. Serve as an hors d'oeuvre.

Beet Salad

Cut the beets into slices; serve them with a dressing made of salad oil, vinegar, salt, pepper, and finely chopped fresh herbs.

This is delicious with boiled beef.

Beet Salad with Horseradish

Follow the recipe for *beet salad*. Add some grated horseradish to the dressing and mix well.

CUCUMBERS

About the only thing cucumbers can be used for is salads.

Cucumber Salad

Peel a cucumber. Cut it in half lengthwise and take the seeds out with a spoon. Cut the cucumber into slices as thin as possible. Sprinkle them with salt and put them into a salad bowl. Place a saucer or small plate on top of the cucumber—it should sit directly on it. Push down hard and put a weight (a bottle full of water, for example) on top of the saucer. Wait 10 minutes so that the water contained in the cucumber can seep out. Then pour the water off and season the cucumber with oil, vinegar, salt, pepper, and chopped herbs.

Cucumbers with Sour Cream

Prepare the cucumber according to the preceding recipe. After you have poured the water off, season the cucumber with salt, very little vinegar, and sour cream.

TOMATOES

Tomatoes can be prepared very quickly, so they are invaluable to ten-minute cooking. They are best when they are in season, that is, during the summer months.

Tomato Salad

The tomatoes you use should be fully ripe. Cut them into slices and season them with olive oil, wine vinegar, salt, pepper, and chopped herbs. In the south of France, a finely chopped clove of garlic is always added. I wouldn't recommend this for more temperate climates.

Tomatoes à la Provençale

Cut 2 tomatoes in half.

Heat some cooking oil in a frying pan, then add 2 shallots and 1 small onion, both finely chopped. Place the tomato halves in the pan flat side down. Cook 5 minutes, then turn the tomatoes over, piercing the skin in a few places with a fork.

Cook the tomatoes 5 minutes more over high heat, then add salt and pepper. Sprinkle with freshly chopped parsley and serve.

Tomatoes Polish Style

Cut 2 tomatoes in two.

Melt some butter in a frying pan and add a finely chopped onion. Place the tomatoes in the pan, flat side down, and cook them on high heat for 5 minutes. Turn them over, piercing the skin here and there with a fork. Cook 5 minutes longer, then sprinkle with salt and pepper. Add 2 generous tablespoons sour cream, placing it between the tomato halves. Bring the sauce barely to a boil; at the first bubble, take off the fire and serve.

SPINACH

Canned spinach can be bought anywhere. Open the can and pour the contents into a colander so the juice can drain off. When you heat it up, make sure you don't use an iron pan; it will turn the spinach black.

Buttered Spinach

Melt a lump of butter in a saucepan, then add the spinach. Stir it around and add salt. When the spinach is hot, serve it with veal, eggs, or fish.

Creamed Spinach

Follow the above recipe, but before serving, add some heavy cream. Stir it in well, and serve when hot.

SORREL

Fresh sorrel melts into a creamy paste when exposed to heat. It is rarely used alone as a vegetable but is a classic accompaniment to veal and fish.

Sorrel with Veal

Wash some sorrel. Melt a lump of butter in a saucepan, then add the sorrel. Stir it around with a wooden spatula as it heats. In 5 minutes the sorrel will have turned into a not-too-appetizing brownish cream. At that point, add it to a fried veal cutlet which has nearly finished cooking. Mix it in with the meat juices that surround the cutlet, add salt, and serve.

MUSHROOMS

Ordinary button mushrooms are the only ones we will be using fresh. They can be easily cleaned, and on top of that, they contain relatively little water. This means that they cook rapidly, since it doesn't take long to evaporate the small amount of water they will give out.

The highly prized cèpe (boletus) can be bought in cans. This mushroom is used for making a traditional French dish called "Cèpes à la Bordelaise."

Mushrooms can be used to garnish meats, eggs, and fish. You can use them as often as you like in ten-minute cooking, since they improve the taste of any dish to which they are added.

Creamed Mushrooms

½ lb. fresh mushrooms	Salt and pepper
2 tbsp. butter	4 tbsp. heavy cream
1 onion, finely chopped	½ tsp. flour

Cut off the sandy end of the mushroom stems, then wash the mushrooms in a big bowl of cold water. Take them out of the bowl, throw away the dirty water and sand, then fill the bowl again with fresh water. Do this 3 times. Cut the mushrooms into thin slices. After that, wash them off one last time and pat them dry in a towel.

Melt the butter in a large saucepan. Add the onion, then the mushrooms. Cover the pot and turn the heat up all the way. Steam is coming out from under the cover; the mushrooms have given out their water and it's boiling. Take the top off the saucepan and let the mushrooms boil rapidly, so that the water will evaporate. Add salt and pepper. After 6 minutes there should be just a little liquid left in the pot. Mix the heavy cream with the flour, and add this mixture to the mushrooms. Stir well, and when the sauce is smooth and creamy, serve. It's divine.

Cèpes à la Bordelaise

Olive oil	1 can of cèpes (boletus mush-
3 shallots, finely chopped	rooms)
1 clove garlic, finely	Salt and pepper
chopped	Fresh parsley

Heat some olive oil in a frying pan. Add the shallots and garlic. Rinse the cèpes in cold water, and place them in the frying pan. Cook for 6 to 7 minutes, then add salt and pepper. Serve sprinkled with freshly chopped parsley.

French-Fried Mushrooms

Lard or cooking oil	3 tbsp. flour
½ lb. fresh mushrooms	Beer
1 egg, beaten	Salt

Place a large pot half filled with lard or cooking oil on the stove.

Cut off the sandy ends of the mushroom stems and wash the mushrooms very thoroughly. Wipe them dry with a towel.

Make a batter with the egg, the flour, and enough beer to form a thick but fluid mixture. Dip the mushrooms into the batter, then drop them one at a time into the smoking fat. Cook them 5 to 6 minutes; then take them out of the pot and let the fat drain off. Salt and serve. They're delicious.

VEGETABLE FLOURS

A certain number of vegetable flours (see Introduction, p. xxiv) are sold which have been steamed before packaging. To prepare a creamy puree, you simply dilute the flour in water, bring the mixture to a boil, and add salt. There are, of course, good vegetable flours and bad ones. The good ones taste like the original vegetable, the bad ones taste like sawdust.

So whatever you do, don't pinch pennies when buying vegetable flours. Buy the most expensive ones to be sure of getting the best.

I suggest using flour made from the following vegetables: green peas, white kidney beans, lentils, and broad beans. An excellent puree can also be made from chestnut flour.

The basic preparation is the same for all these flours.

Put 2 generous tablespoons of vegetable flour into a pot. Dilute it with a little cold water, just enough to make a mixture that is barely liquid but will pour. Don't add too much, or the puree will be too runny.

Place the pot on the fire, add salt, and stir quickly while the puree thickens. At a certain point, the puree will puff up and pop, like a tiny volcano. Lower the heat, add a lump of butter, and let it melt. Wait 3 or 4 minutes. Now the puree is ready. Taste to see if it needs more salt, and add a little hot water if you think it is too thick. But be careful. If you add too much water, the puree will have a horrible watery taste.

Green-Pea Puree

Follow the general directions given above and prepare a green-pea puree. Add a lump of butter. For a classical French dish, serve it with chitterling sausages (andouillettes).

Or, if you prefer, instead of adding butter, add some bacon which has been cut into little pieces and fried.

Lentil Puree

Follow the directions given above, using lentil-flour puree.

This puree is very good with breakfast sausages or flat sausage patties. Pour the fat from the sausages over the puree.

White-Bean Puree

Follow the directions given above and make a white-bean puree. This is an excellent accompaniment to *fried pork chops*.

Chestnut Puree

Make a puree following the basic technique described above, but add very little water to start. You can add more later if necessary. Add a large lump of butter and a lot of salt, but pepper very lightly.

Serve chestnut puree with *fried pork chops*; pour the fat from the pork chops over the puree. And put some good, hot Dijon mustard on the table.

Broad-Bean Puree

Make a broad-bean puree following the general directions given for vegetable flours. Serve it with salt pork which has already been cooked. Heat the pork up in a little boiling water, then serve surrounded by the puree.

SOME QUICK
BUT REFINED
MEAT DISHES

Beef is ideal for ten-minute cooking, since it is best when served rare.

All the following recipes are for two people.

Rib Steak with French-Fried Potatoes

Put a pot half filled with oil on the stove and make some *French-fried potatoes.*

While the potatoes are cooking, melt a very small lump of butter in a frying pan. When the butter begins to smoke, place a 10½-ounce rib steak in the pan. Wait 3 minutes, turn it over, then wait 3 more minutes. Salt the meat and put it on a serving platter. Sprinkle a little

chopped parsley over the steak and slip a fresh lump of butter underneath it. Serve it with the French fries.

Rib Steak with Onions

Cook a 10½-ounce rib steak as in the preceding recipe, but place 1 finely chopped onion in the pan around the steak. The onion will brown with the steak. Serve the steak with the onion on top.

Rib Steak à la Minute

Butter   1 shallot, chopped
1 10½-oz. rib steak   Ham
¼ lb. fresh mushrooms, thinly
    sliced

Cook the steak as directed on p. 100. While the steak is browning, melt some butter in another pan and add the mushrooms and the shallot. Cook them over a very hot burner so that the water given off by the mushrooms will evaporate. When all the water is gone, pour the mushrooms into the pan with the steak. Just before serving, add some small pieces of ham and mix everything together.

Serve the steak surrounded by its garnish.

Rib Steak Béarnaise

Cook a 10½-ounce rib steak as directed on p. 100. While your steak is cooking on one burner, prepare *béarnaise sauce* on another. Follow the recipe for béarnaise sauce, but use just 1 egg yolk and 5 tablespoons butter, as that will make plenty of sauce for this dish. Spoon the sauce over the steak and serve.

Fillet Steak with Sautéed Potatoes

Cut some cooked potatoes in slices, and sauté them in butter.

In another frying pan, heat some butter until it smokes. Put a 9-ounce fillet steak in the pan and cook it for 3 minutes over very high heat. Turn the steak over and cook it for 3 more minutes; then sprinkle it with salt.

Serve the steak on a hot platter with the sautéed potatoes around it, and enjoy yourself.

Fillet Steaks with Madeira

Put a little butter in a frying pan, and when it is very hot, place 2 fillet steaks in the pan. Cook 3 minutes on each side, then sprinkle with salt. Arrange the fillets on a hot platter. Pour 2 tablespoons Madeira into the frying pan and bring to a boil. Pour this sauce over the steaks and serve.

Fillet Steaks Dauphinoise

Prepare ¼ pound mushrooms according to the recipe for *creamed mushrooms*.

In a second frying pan make *fillet steaks with Madeira*. To serve, pour the mushrooms into a serving dish, place the steaks on top of them, and pour the Madeira sauce over them.

Fillet Steaks Rossini

Follow the recipe for *fillet steaks with Madeira*, but when you make the sauce, add some bits of truffle to it.

When the steaks are cooked, place them on a serving platter. Lay a slice of *foie gras truffé* on each filet steak. Each slice should be as big around as the steak in order to cover it completely. Pour the Madeira-truffle sauce over the steaks. This is a dish for very special occasions.

A Good, Plain Steak

Not every day is a special occasion, and sometimes it's nice to have a good, plain steak.

Buy a 10-ounce steak cut from the flank or sirloin.

Heat some butter in a frying pan until it smokes, then add your steak. Cook it 3 minutes on one side, 3 minutes on the other, then serve sprinkled with salt and garnished with parsley and *French-fried potatoes*.

Bitocks à la Russe

¼ cup stale bread	Butter
½ lb. ground beef	White wine
Salt and pepper	Cognac
1 egg yolk	

Soak the stale bread in a little water and squeeze it dry. Mix the meat and bread together with your fingers; add salt, pepper, and the egg yolk. Make 4 thick meatballs, slightly flattened on the top and bottom. Fry them in butter, 4 minutes on each side, then take them out of the frying pan. Pour into the pan a little white wine and a tiny bit of cognac. Stir this sauce until all the meat juices have dissolved in it, then pour it over the bitocks.

These bitocks are best with noodles which have been cooked in boiling salted water and tossed with butter.

VEAL

It's understood that braised veal roasts and slowly simmered stews are out of the question for ten-minute cooking. We will be limited to veal scallops and cutlets. But, as you will see, a variety of interesting dishes can be made with them.

Fried Veal Scallops

This is the easiest thing in the world to make.

1. Pour some flour onto a plate. Take 2 veal scallops and roll them in the flour until they are completely covered. Pat the flour into them with your fingers. None of this should be done, however, until you have placed a frying pan on the fire. If you flour the scallops too far in advance, the moisture from the meat will penetrate the flour and make it sticky.

2. Put a lump of butter into your hot frying pan. When the butter begins to smoke, place the veal scallops in the pan, and let them cook for 2 minutes. Then turn them over and let them cook for 2 minutes on the other side. Now turn them over again and cook them for 3 minutes more on the first side.

This may seem like a useless ritual, but it's not. If

you wait too long before turning the meat over the first time, the flour on top of the meat will be moistened by the juices which are seeping out of the meat. Then, when you turn it over, the wet layer of flour will detach from the meat and your scallop will not brown correctly.

When the scallops are nicely browned on both sides, salt them, take them out of the pan, and place them on a hot platter. Pour a little water into the frying pan and bring it to a boil. The water will dissolve the caramelized meat juices stuck to the pan and make a nice brown sauce which you will pour over your veal.

Serve the scallops with *noodles English style,* which you have prepared while the veal was cooking.

Veal Scallops with Olives

Follow the preceding recipe. Buy some pitted green olives, or pit them yourself, and 3 minutes before the scallops are done, add the olives to the frying pan. When the veal is done, remove it from the pan, but leave the olives. Pour 2 tablespoons hot water into the frying pan and let the sauce and olives boil for 1 minute; then pour over the scallops placed on a hot platter.

Serve this dish garnished with a few lettuce leaves that have been seasoned with oil, vinegar, salt, and pepper.

Veal Scallops with Tomato Sauce

Follow the recipe for *fried veal scallops,* but when making the sauce, add a teaspoon of tomato paste. Mix the veal juices and tomato paste until smooth, cook for 1 minute, then pour this beautiful red sauce over the veal scallops and serve.

Veal Scallops Spanish Style

Follow the preceding recipe. When you are making the sauce, add some pitted black olives along with the tomato paste. Heat the sauce and olives; then pour over the scallops and serve.

Veal Scallops Magyar

Follow the recipe for *fried veal scallops*. When you are making the sauce, add some paprika. Serve the scallops with *Alsatian dumplings*, which you can make while the scallops are cooking.

Veal Scallops Bordelaise

Follow the recipe for *fried veal scallops*. On another burner, prepare some *cèpes à la bordelaise*, or use fresh button mushrooms and cook them with olive oil and shallots.

Serve the fried scallops surrounded by the mushrooms.

Veal Scallops with Cream Sauce

Follow the recipe for *fried veal scallops*. When making the brown sauce, add 2 tablespoons heavy cream to it. Mix well, bring to a boil, and pour over the veal scallops. Serve with *buttered green peas*, which you have prepared on another burner while the scallops were cooking.

Veal Scallops with Capers

Follow the recipe for *fried veal scallops*. Add to the sauce 1 teaspoon capers, and pour over the scallops when hot.

Veal Scallops Zingara

Follow the recipe for *fried veal scallops*. In a second frying pan, brown some finely sliced fresh mushrooms, then add some chopped ham and a few bits of truffle. When this mixture is hot, add it to the sauce in the scallop pan. Bring to a boil and pour over the scallops. It's delicious.

Wiener Schnitzel

Lard or cooking oil	2 very thin veal scallops
Flour	Salt
1 egg, beaten	Lemon slices
Bread crumbs	

Put a pot half filled with cooking oil or lard on the stove. (Don't use beef fat, as it is good only for *French-fried potatoes.*)

Arrange 3 plates in front of you. The first should contain flour, the second the egg, and the third some bread crumbs.

Have the butcher flatten the veal scallops *as much as he can.* With a knife, cut little slits all around the edge of each scallop.

Roll the scallops in (1) flour, (2) egg, (3) bread crumbs. Drop them into the smoking fat. Let them cook until they are golden brown—about 6 minutes—then take them out of the pot, sprinkle with salt, and place on a hot platter. Serve decorated with slices of lemon.

Fried Veal Cutlets

Cook 2 veal cutlets as you would *fried veal scallops.* It isn't absolutely necessary to roll them in flour, however.

Floured or not, brown them in butter in a frying pan. Dissolve the meat glaze left in the pan with either water or white wine, and pour this sauce over the cutlets.

All the recipes for veal scallops can be applied to veal cutlets.

Veal Cutlets Milanese Style

Prepare the cutlets as you would veal scallops for *Wiener schnitzel*—that is, roll them in (1) flour, (2) egg, (3) bread crumbs.

Fry them in smoking hot butter. When they're done, sprinkle with salt. When serving, add a little fresh butter to the butter the cutlets cooked in, and when it has melted, pour over the meat.

Veal Cutlets Pojarski

¼ cup stale bread	2 eggs
Milk	Flour
½ lb. ground veal	Bread crumbs
Salt and pepper	Butter

Theoretically, these cutlets, which are really meatballs made of white meat, are prepared with chicken. In practice, they are made most often with veal.

Soak the stale bread in a little milk, squeeze out the moisture, and mix the bread with the veal. Add salt, pepper, and the yolk of 1 egg, mixing everything together with your fingers.

Make patties that are the size and thickness of the meaty part of a veal cutlet, then roll them in (1) flour, (2) a beaten egg, (3) bread crumbs. Fry them for 8 to 10 minutes in very hot butter.

Serve your cutlets Pojarski with *buttered green peas*, prepared on another burner while your cutlets are cooking.

L A M B

Lamb is well suited for ten-minute cooking since it is excellent served rare. Only the most tender cuts should be used: rib lamb chops, leg steaks, loin lamb chops.

Broiled Lamb Chops

As soon as you walk into the house, with your hat still on your head, go to the kitchen and light the broiler. Open the window, too.

Melt a little butter in a saucepan, and with a basting brush, coat the lamb chops with it.

When the broiler is good and hot—that is, after pre-heating for 5 minutes—place the lamb chops on the broiler grill and slide them under the flame. After 3 minutes, turn them over and cook 3 more minutes on the other side; then sprinkle with salt.

Serve your lamb chops with *French-fried potatoes*, made while the lamb chops were under the broiler.

Fried Lamb Chops

Lamb chops are fried like steaks—that is, in a little butter for 3 minutes on each side. Salt when done, and serve with *French-fried potatoes*.

Lamb Steaks

Buy some slices of lamb cut from the upper end of a leg of lamb. These are sometimes referred to as leg steaks. They can either be fried or broiled, like lamb chops. Serve them with *French-fried potatoes*.

Loin Lamb Chops

If you prefer, you can buy loin lamb chops, which have less bone than rib chops. Cook them as you would rib chops, broiled or fried, and serve with *French-fried potatoes*.

Breaded Lamb Steaks

Roll leg-of-lamb steaks in (1) flour, (2) beaten egg, (3) bread crumbs. Fry them in butter and serve with good, hot Dijon mustard.

Lamb Sautéed American Style

Buy 2 steaks cut from the upper end of a leg of lamb. Cut each steak into 4 pieces.

Cut 3 slices of good bacon into very small squares.

In a frying pan (1) melt some butter, (2) brown the bacon, (3) add the pieces of lamb. Sauté for 6 to 7 minutes in the hot bacon fat. Salt very lightly and serve immediately on a hot platter.

Lamb Georgian Style

Buy 2 steaks cut from the upper end of a leg of lamb. Cut each one into 4 pieces and sauté the meat in butter in a frying pan. Add salt and pepper; then sprinkle a little wine vinegar over the meat. When the vinegar has evaporated, serve the steaks with a few slices of raw onion on top. Traditionally this dish is eaten with the fingers.

PORK

Pork chops and steaks, breaded pig's feet, ears, snouts, and tails are delicious treats offered by the noble pig to people who are in a hurry. Their artful preparation is up to you.

Fried Pork Chops

Don't buy pork chops that are too thick. They won't have the time to cook completely; pork should always be eaten well done.

Melt a small lump of butter in a frying pan. Place 2 pork chops in the pan and turn up the heat as high as possible. The fat on the meat will begin to melt, and the chops will brown rapidly. Cook them for 5 minutes on one side, then 5 minutes on the other; they will be cooked to perfection. Sprinkle with salt and serve with hot Dijon mustard. This is the easiest way to cook pork chops. There's no reason to complicate it, and the fat the pork chops give off can be used as a sauce for the meat.

Pork Chops and Applesauce

Peel some good-quality cooking apples, tart but not sour, and remove the core and seeds. Cut them into small pieces, then place them in a saucepan with very little water. Put the pot on the fire, cover it, and bring to a boil. After 5 minutes, mash the apples with a spoon. If the apples are of good quality, they should have turned to applesauce after a total of 10 minutes' cooking time. Sprinkle the applesauce with salt and pepper.

While the apples are cooking, prepare 2 *fried pork chops*. Put them on a serving platter and surround with the applesauce. Pour the melted pork fat from the frying pan over the applesauce, and serve with hot Dijon mustard.

Pork Chops with Onion

Chop a large onion into fine pieces. Heat some butter in a frying pan, and when it's very hot, add 2 pork chops. Two minutes later, add the onion. Cook the meat as usual, but stir the onion into the melting pork fat every minute or so. Salt, and serve with good, hot Dijon mustard.

Pork Chops and Noodles

Make *noodles English style.*

Meanwhile, prepare some *fried pork chops.* Place the pork chops on a platter with the noodles. Pour the fat from the pan over the noodles and serve.

Pork Chops and Sautéed Potatoes

Peel some boiled potatoes, and cut them into slices. Heat some lard in a frying pan, and when it is smoking hot, add the potatoes.

While they are cooking, follow the recipe for *fried pork chops.* At the last minute, add the sautéed potatoes, stir them into the fat from the pork chops, and serve.

Pork Chops Italian Style

Cook some noodles according to the recipe for *noodles English style.* During the ten minutes they're cooking, make some *fried pork chops.*

When the pork chops are done, add to the fat in the pan a teaspoon of tomato paste, with enough water to make the sauce just slightly runny. Place the pork chops on a platter, pour the tomato sauce over them, and garnish the dish with the buttered noodles.

Pork Chops with Chestnut Puree

On one burner of your stove, make some *chestnut puree*. On another burner, fry 2 pork chops.

Arrange the pork chops on a platter surrounded by the puree. Pour the fat from the pork chops over everything, and serve.

Pork Chops with White Beans

Fry 2 pork chops. Halfway through their cooking time, add a drained can of white kidney beans. Stir the beans into the meat juice, finish cooking, and serve.

Pork Chops and Sauerkraut

On one burner, reheat some sauerkraut which has already been cooked. On another burner, prepare 2 *fried pork chops*.

Place the pork chops on a platter with the sauerkraut around them. Pour the fat from the pork chops over the sauerkraut, and serve.

Fried Pork Steaks

What I am calling pork steaks are boneless slices of pork, taken from a roasting cut. These steaks are excellent when fried, as the outside quickly becomes crisp in smoking butter or lard. Sprinkle with salt and pepper, and serve with hot Dijon mustard.

Pork Steaks Fried in Bread Crumbs

2 pork steaks	Bread crumbs
Flour	Butter or lard
1 egg, beaten	Salt and pepper

Roll some pork steaks in (1) flour, (2) egg, (3) bread crumbs. Fry the steaks in smoking butter or lard. Serve as they are, ungarnished, but sprinkle generously with salt and pepper.

Breaded Pig's Feet

Cooked breaded pig's feet can be bought in any good charcuterie. They are usually sold cut in half lengthwise.

Pig's feet can be fried in smoking butter or lard, but this is dangerous. The bread-crumb crust almost always splits. The hot fat flies all over.

A better solution is to roll them in a little cooking oil and cook them under the broiler. That way it doesn't matter if the fat splatters.

Since the feet are rather thick, it will take 10 minutes for them to heat through. Serve them with hot Dijon mustard. This is an excellent dish, even though it is a little hard to eat, especially if you don't want to leave any meat on the bones. You'll dirty your fingers as much as your mouth . . . but it's worth it.

Breaded Pig's Ears

The same observations and preparation apply here as for pig's feet. Roll the ears in cooking oil and broil them. Serve with hot Dijon mustard.

Breaded Pigs' Tails

Cooked, breaded pigs' tails should be prepared like breaded pig's feet and ears. Unforunately, you don't see them for sale very often. It is true that each pig has only one tail for two ears and eight half feet . . . maybe that's why.

THE FRENCH CHARCUTERIE

In a good French charcuterie, you will find the makings of a very quick lunch. Some of the products can be eaten cold, such as: ham, smoked sausages, jellied calf's head, galantines, liver patés, rillons, rillettes, not to mention the luxury products like foie gras truffé and patés of venison, hare, and pheasant.

You can make a main dish of any or all of these preparations. Serve an omelet first, then your charcuterie selection accompanied by a green salad; follow that by some cheese and fruit, and you will have made a most enviable meal.

A charcuterie also sells a certain number of dishes which can be easily reheated, so take advantage of the invaluable resources it offers to ten-minute cooking.

Sautéed Ham

Heat some butter in a frying pan, and when it's smoking hot, add a slice of ham. Cook it for 2 minutes on each side. Serve it with *sautéed potatoes* or *buttered green peas* prepared while the ham is cooking. In the chapter on eggs, you learned about *ham and eggs*. That's delicious too.

Crépinette Sausages and Saucisses Longues

There are two basic shapes for sausages. A "crépinette" is a sausage patty made of sausage meat wrapped in a pig's caul (a very thin membrane laced with white fat). "Saucisses longues" (long breakfast sausages) are made of the same stuffing but have the traditional sausage shape. Both kinds of sausage are cooked the same way.

Heat some butter over a medium fire until it smokes, then place the sausages in the pan. Prick their skins here and there with a pin or fork before cooking them.

Cook the sausages for 5 minutes on one side; then turn them over and let them cook 5 minutes more. Put them on a hot platter, and heat up some canned white kidney beans or some baby limas in the sausage fat left in the pan. Serve the sausages with the beans—they're delicious.

Sausages are also excellent with *green-pea puree*.

Toulouse Sausage

The Toulouse sausage looks like a breakfast sausage, but it is much longer and thicker. A really good one is made, not with mechanically ground meat, but with lean and fat pork chopped up with a knife. It therefore takes much longer to cook it—a good 15 minutes.

Prick the sausage all over with a fork to keep the skin from splitting when it cooks, then fry it in smoking butter.

Five minutes before the sausage is done, add some canned white kidney beans and sauté them with the sausage until done.

Chipolatas

Chipolatas are small link sausages. Cook them like crépinette (flat) sausages in a pan with smoking butter.

Chipolatas can be served with sautéed white kidney beans or hot sauerkraut. They are also very good with *French-fried eggs* or *tomato sauce*.

Strasbourg Sausages and Frankfurters

These two sausages have certain things in common, and they are both cooked in boiling water. But real Frankfurter sausages have much more taste—for that matter, they are much more expensive.

Put the sausages into a pot of cold water, then put the pot on the burner. When you see that the water is just beginning to boil, lower the flame and leave the sausages for 10 minutes. They should cook at a temperature around 190° F.; if you let them boil, their skins might split.

Take the sausages out of the water and serve them with either potato salad or hot sauerkraut. The first combination is the most traditional.

To eat your sausage, pick it up with the tips of your fingers and bite off the end. Above all, never prick it with your fork; the juice will run out and all will be lost.

Boiled Cervelats

Cervelats (saveloy sausages) are prepared like Strasbourg sausages and Frankfurters, but you don't have to be so careful with them. Their skin is much tougher, so you can let them boil rapidly for 7 to 8 minutes.

They are best served with *potato salad*. When it's in season, chopped tarragon is a nice addition to the salad.

One cervelat per person is plenty.

Broiled Cervelats

Take 2 cervelats (saveloy sausages) and remove the skins. This is easy if you slit them with a very sharp knife.

Cut each sausage in two lengthwise. Place them on a plate with their flat side down. On the rounded side, make a criss-cross design with the tip of your knife, just barely penetrating the surface of the meat.

Place the four half sausages on the broiler grill with the rounded side facing up. Broil for 8 to 10 minutes.

Serve the cervelats with *buttered spinach*, prepared while the sausages are under the broiler.

Fried Boudin

Buy some good boudin (blood sausage); good boudin is hard to find, even in Paris. Cut it into pieces 4–5 inches long. On each side of each piece, make 3 slits with a sharp knife. Melt some butter in a frying pan, and when it's smoking, add the sausage. Cook over a high fire.

Serve with *sautéed potatoes* or with applesauce made according to the recipe for *pork chops and applesauce*. And don't forget to serve blood sausage with hot Dijon mustard.

Andouillettes

The best chitterling sausages are the andouillettes de Troyes, which are encased in gelatin and sold in any good French charcuterie.

Cut a few slits in the skin, then fry the andouillettes in butter. When they are golden brown and very hot, serve them with *chestnut puree* or *white-bean puree*.

Salt Pork

If you can find salt pork which has already been cooked, you should buy it often.

Put the pork into a pot and half-cover it with boiling water. Cover the pot and let the pork boil for 6 to 7 minutes—just long enough to heat it thoroughly.

Serve the salt pork with canned white kidney beans sautéed in butter.

TRIPE, ETC.

Precooked tripe, sold in glass jars, is a product appreciated by both people in a hurry and gourmets. One does not exclude the other, although it is said that a gourmet always eats slowly—almost religiously.

Modern life has changed the rhythm of things, and often one meets gourmets who have to content themselves with meals which are rapidly prepared and, regretfully, rapidly eaten. But that doesn't mean they're not gourmets.

In Paris the only kind of precooked tripe you find is
"Tripes à la mode de Caen," a wonderful dish which is
one of the glories of French cuisine.

Tripes à la Mode de Caen

Buy some precooked "Tripes à la mode de Caen." Make
sure you buy a good brand. It consists of pieces of beef
stomach encased in solid gelatin. The gelatin is made
from calf's feet. A pound of tripe is more than enough
for two people.

Put the block of tripe into a small pot and add a tablespoon of water. Place the pot on the stove, stirring constantly so that the gelatin will melt without sticking to
the bottom of the pot. When it has melted and the
pieces of tripe float freely in the liquid, lower the heat,
cover the pot, and cook the tripe for 7 to 8 minutes more.
Serve with hot Dijon mustard.

If you want to make this fabulous dish even better, add
a tablespoon of apple brandy or Calvados to the tripe as
soon as it has melted. After boiling for 5 minutes, most
of the alcohol will have evaporated, but a delicate taste
has been added to the tripe.

Sautéed Honeycomb Tripe

Honeycomb tripe is usually sold already cooked and
rolled up. Half a pound is plenty for two people.

Cut the tripe into squares. Sauté them quickly in very
hot butter, just long enough to heat them thoroughly.
Sprinkle with salt, pepper, and chopped parsley.

Be sure to serve hot Dijon mustard and drink a cold white wine with this dish.

Honeycomb Tripe with Tomato Sauce

Follow the recipe for *tomato sauce*, but make the sauce quite thick.

Cover some *sautéed honeycomb tripe* with the sauce and serve.

Lambs' Brains with Black Butter

Lambs' brains are always cleaned before being sold.

Fill a pot with water and season it with salt, vinegar, a bay leaf, allspice, etc. Bring the water to a boil, rinse the lambs' brains in cold water, and drop them into the boiling, seasoned water. Cook them for 10 minutes.

Meanwhile, brown some butter in a frying pan. Let it cool off a little, then add a few drops of vinegar and salt. Take the brains out of the pot and place them on a towel to drain for a few seconds. Then arrange them on a plate, pour the hot butter over them, sprinkle with bread crumbs, and serve.

Skewered Lambs' Kidneys

Buy some lambs' kidneys and ask the butcher to split them open for you. When you get home, run a small skewer through each one so they will remain open and not curl up while they're cooking.

Brown some butter in a frying pan, then add the

skewered kidneys. Sauté them for 4 minutes on one side; then turn them over and cook them for 4 minutes more. Sprinkle with salt and chopped parsley, and serve with *French-fried potatoes*.

Broiled Lambs' Kidneys

Have the butcher split open the lambs' kidneys for you. Run them onto small skewers and use a basting brush to coat them with cooking oil.

Preheat the broiler for 5 minutes, then place the kidneys on the grill under the heat. Cook them for 5 minutes on each side.

Make some *French-fried potatoes* while the kidneys are cooking. Serve the kidneys with fresh watercress and the French fries.

Beef Kidneys Béarnaise

Beef kidneys are underrated. It's really too bad.

Buy 10½ ounces of beef kidney for two people. Cut it into slices 1 inch thick.

Fry the slices of kidney in butter, like steaks. Eight minutes will be long enough to cook them through. Sprinkle with salt and pepper.

While the meat is cooking, make some *béarnaise sauce*. Pour the sauce over the sliced kidney and serve. Absolutely delicious.

Sautéed Veal Kidneys

Buy 8 ounces of veal kidney for two servings. I'm warning you, it's very expensive. Cut it into pieces about ¾ inch square. Clean ¼ pound mushrooms and cut them into slices. Don't peel them.

Brown some butter in a frying pan, then add the pieces of kidney. Cook them for 5 minutes, then add the mushrooms, salt, and pepper. Cook over very high heat until all the water given off by the mushrooms has evaporated. Serve on a hot platter.

Veal Kidneys with Port

Make some *sautéed veal kidneys*. Add 3 tablespoons of port when you add the mushrooms. Serve when half the liquid has evaporated.

Flambéed Veal Kidneys

Make some *sautéed veal kidneys*. Add 1 tablespoon good cognac when you add the mushrooms. Light the cognac in the frying pan with a match; then continue with the rest of the recipe. Serve as is, ungarnished.

Veal Kidneys with Cream

Make some *sautéed veal kidneys*. Just before serving, add ⅓ cup heavy cream mixed with ½ teaspoon flour. Mix everything together well and bring to a boil. Add salt and pepper, then serve. It's divine.

Veal Kidneys with Mustard

If you like spicy dishes, try this one. Make *veal kidneys with cream*, but add a generous teaspoon of very good, hot Dijon mustard when you add the cream. After that, simply continue as described above.

Sautéed Calf's Liver

Calf's liver may break the bank, but it's good. Beef liver is much less expensive, but it can't compare to calf's liver. Calf's liver stays tender after being cooked, beef liver tends to curl and get tough, so it has to be cooked as little as possible. Use whichever you prefer.

Take 2 slices of liver weighing approximately 5 ounces each. They mustn't be cut too thin, because the inside should still be pink after it's cooked.

Roll the liver slices in flour, then fry them in smoking butter. Cook them 3 minutes on one side, 4 minutes on the other, then add salt. Pour a few drops of vinegar into the frying pan and add a lump of butter. When the butter has melted, place the liver on a serving platter and pour the butter over it. Sprinkle with some chopped parsley and serve.

Sautéed Calf's Liver with Cream

Make 2 slices of *sautéed calf's liver*. Before serving, add ⅓ cup heavy cream; mix with the butter, pour the sauce over the liver, and serve. Don't add parsley.

Calf's Liver Fried in Bread Crumbs

2 slices calf's liver	Bread crumbs
Flour	Butter
1 egg, beaten	2 lemon slices

You must use only calf's liver for this recipe. Roll the liver in (1) flour, (2) egg, (3) bread crumbs. Fry them in butter which is hot but not smoking.

Cook liver 4 minutes on each side. Serve each slice of liver with a slice of lemon.

Liver American Style

1 12½-oz. slice beef liver	Paprika
4 slices bacon	Salt
Butter	Cheddar cheese (optional)

Cut the liver into pieces about 1 inch square. Chop the bacon into small pieces.

Melt some butter in a frying pan and add the bacon. Fry it for 5 minutes, then add the liver. Let everything brown together for 5 minutes, then sprinkle with paprika.

Salt very lightly since the bacon may be quite salty itself.

You can serve this dish either as it is or with slices of Cheddar cheese.

POULTRY

You won't be able to cook a chicken—or even a squab—in ten minutes. So resign yourself to buying chickens (or half chickens) which are sold already roasted.

This doesn't mean that the only way you can eat chicken is cold and sprinkled with salt. You can reheat it and make different kinds of "salmis" or stews. Here are a few of the numerous possibilities.

Cold Chicken with Mayonnaise

Simply serve the roasted chicken with *mayonnaise*. The mayonnaise doesn't take long to make and the two go very well together.

Chicken Sautéed with Mushrooms

1 small roast chicken	¼ lb. fresh mushrooms
Butter	⅓ cup white wine
1 onion, finely chopped	½ tsp. meat extract
3 slices bacon, chopped	Salt

Cut the chicken into 8 pieces: 2 legs, 2 wings, 2 breasts, and the rest of the body cut in two.

Melt some butter in a heavy casserole and add the

onion and bacon. Brown over high heat for 2 minutes, then add the mushrooms, thinly sliced, and the chicken. Add the white wine mixed with the meat extract. Cover the pot and cook over high heat for 7 to 8 minutes. Taste and add salt if necessary. Everything's ready. Serve it in the casserole or in a warm serving dish.

Chicken with Sour Cream

Butter	1 small roast chicken
3 slices bacon, chopped	⅓ cup water
1 onion, finely chopped	1 tsp. meat extract
¼ lb. fresh mushrooms, thinly sliced	4 tbsp. sour cream
	½ tsp. flour

As in the preceding recipe, melt some butter in a casserole and brown the bacon, the onion, and the mushrooms. Add the roast chicken cut into 8 pieces. Pour over it the water mixed with the meat extract.

Before serving, add the sour cream mixed with the flour. Stir the cream quickly into the sauce and bring it barely to a boil. At the first bubble, take the pot off the heat and serve.

Chicken Marengo

Follow the recipe for *chicken sautéed with mushrooms*, but before adding the white wine, mix it carefully with a tablespoon of tomato paste. Otherwise, do everything as described above. It's ready.

Chicken Paprika

Follow the recipe for *chicken with sour cream*, but at the beginning of the recipe, add 1 teaspoon of paprika to the other ingredients.

Foie Gras

You won't have time to make a foie gras yourself, so buy it already prepared (with or without a pastry shell). You can buy good foie gras with truffles by the slice at any good charcuterie. Excellent foies gras are also sold in small earthenware dishes.

Don't do anything to change the taste of your foie gras. Eat it just as it is, with nothing more than a lettuce leaf to garnish it.

GAME

You will be eating neither hare nor rabbit stew, nor woodcock salmis. But if we think about it a little, we can find a number of game dishes that can be added to your menus and that merit the praise of a real gourmet.

Larks en Cocotte

Buy 4 larks which have already been plucked, cleaned, and wrapped in fat or bacon. Melt some butter in a small earthenware casserole and place the larks in the pan side by side. Brown on one side over a hot fire for 4 minutes, then turn them over. Cook them for another 6

minutes. When they're done, salt them and put them aside on a hot plate. Brown 4 slices of stale bread in the fat left in the pan. Place the larks on these "croutons" and serve.

Quail en Cocotte

A quail is a little too big to cook through in 10 minutes. It takes at least 15. In order not to waste time, buy a quail which has already been plucked and cleaned. With a large pair of scissors, cut the quail down the backbone. Open it up and flatten it with a rolling pin. Brown it in butter in an earthenware casserole. Cooked in this way, it will be ready in 10 minutes.

Quail à la Crapaudine

Open a quail and flatten it according to the directions in the preceding recipe.

Roll it in (1) flour, (2) a beaten egg, (3) bread crumbs. Brown it in butter the way you would *veal cutlets Milanese style*. Sprinkle with salt and add a lump of fresh butter to the butter the quail cooked in. When the butter has melted, pour it over the quail and serve.

Venison Cutlets

Fry some venison cutlets as you would lamb chops. When they are done, dissolve the meat glaze left in the frying pan with 3 tablespoons white wine and 1 tablespoon cognac. Boil this sauce for 3 minutes, then pour it over the cutlets. Serve with *chestnut puree*.

Saddle of Hare with Sour Cream

2 slices saddle of hare	2 tbsp. dry white wine
Butter	1 tsp. flour
Salt and pepper	2 generous tbsp. sour cream

Fry the hare steaks for 10 minutes in smoking butter, then salt and pepper lightly. Pour the wine into the frying pan and boil it for 2 minutes. Mix the flour with the sour cream; then stir this mixture into the sauce in the pan. Bring just barely to a boil—at the first bubble, take the pan off the fire.

Place the hare steaks on a serving platter and pour

the sauce over them. Garnish the dish with chopped beets which have been sautéed in butter and seasoned with a few drops of vinegar.

SOME RARE
TEN-MINUTE
DESSERTS

There are a number of desserts which can be prepared in ten minutes. If it is something that has to cool off before you eat it, make it as soon as you get up in the morning and put it in the ice box so it will be cold at lunchtime. Other quickly prepared desserts are served hot, and these can be made at the last minute.

Here are a few ideas.

French Toast

Dip some slices of stale bread first in milk which has been sweetened with sugar and then in a beaten egg. Fry the bread in butter for 4 minutes on each side.

Serve the French toast with either powdered sugar or jam.

Omelet Flambé

Make an omelet. When it is on the serving platter, sprinkle it with sugar and pour over it a little kirsch, cognac, or rum which has been heated until it is just warm. Light the liquor with a match and serve.

Six Crepes

1 egg
3 tbsp. flour
Milk
Salt

1 tsp. cognac
Butter
Sugar

Break the egg into a large bowl. Add the flour and mix the two together well. This will make a very thick batter. Add milk little by little until the batter forms a creamy liquid but is still thick enough to coat the spoon lightly. Add a tiny bit of salt and the cognac.

Heat a frying pan and grease it by tying a piece of butter inside a little piece of thin cloth and rubbing the pan with the cloth. Using a ladle, pour a little of the batter into the pan, tipping the pan from side to side in order to cover the bottom completely with a thin coating of batter.

Put the pan back on the heat for 5 to 6 seconds. Give the pan a little jerk to loosen the crepe, then turn the crepe over. Cook it for 20 seconds, then remove it from the pan. Make a second crepe, then four others, the same way.

Roll up each crepe when you take it out of the pan.

When they are all ready, melt a large lump of butter in the frying pan and lay the crepes side by side in the pan. Brown them very lightly on one side, then on the other. Put them on a serving platter, sprinkle them with sugar, and serve.

Once you're an expert, you will be able to do all this easily in ten minutes.

Crepes Flambées

Follow the preceding recipe. After sprinkling the crepes with sugar, pour over them a little kirsch or cognac which has been slightly heated in a small saucepan. Light the liquor with a match and serve the crepes with or without jam.

Apple Fritters

Lard or cooking oil	Beer
1 or 2 apples	Salt
1 egg	1 tbsp. kirsch
4 tbsp. flour	Sugar

Put a pot half filled with fat or cooking oil on the stove. Core and peel the apples, then cut them into circular slices.

Break the egg into a bowl and add the flour to it. Beat the egg and flour with a wire whisk. Add beer little by little until you have a batter which is liquid but still thick enough to completely coat a slice of apple dipped into it. Add a little salt and the kirsch to the batter, stirring well.

When the fat or cooking oil begins to smoke, dip the apple slices into the batter, then drop them into the hot fat. Cook for 3 minutes, then remove from pot. Drain off the fat and sprinkle with sugar. They're all ready.

Acacia Flower Fritters

When they're blooming, pick several bunches of acacia flowers and dip them in a fritter batter like that for *apple fritters*. Deep fry them in lard and sprinkle with sugar when done.

Strawberry Fritters

Take some fresh strawberries and dip them one by one into a fritter batter made according to the recipe for *apple fritters*. Deep fry them in lard and sprinkle with sugar before serving.

Banana Fritters

Cut some bananas in half lengthwise. Dip them in a fritter batter made as described for *apple fritters*. Deep fry them in lard. Drain off the fat and serve sprinkled with sugar.

Sautéed Bananas

Cut some bananas in half lengthwise. Sauté them in butter for a few minutes. Serve sprinkled with sugar which has been mixed with a little powdered cinnamon.

Coeur à la Crème with Pineapple

Beat some heavy cream into some farmer's cheese or soft cream cheese with a wire whisk. Add sugar and a little kirsch.

Place some canned pineapple slices on top of the cheese. You can serve this dessert with or without macaroons.

Coeur à la Crème with Cinnamon

Beat some heavy cream into farmer's cheese or soft cream cheese. Stir in some sugar and a little powdered cinnamon. This is a super-quick dessert and it's excellent. You can serve it either with or without vanilla wafers.

Coeur à la Crème with Jam

Beat some farmer's cheese or soft cream cheese together with heavy cream and sugar. Serve it with raspberry or strawberry jam spread over the top.

Fruit Salad

Cut into pieces the following fruits: apples, pears, pineapple, bananas, oranges. When they're in season, add fresh strawberries. Sprinkle the fruit with sugar, pour some white wine over it, and add a tablespoon of kirsch or cognac. For a nice change, you can replace the white wine with maraschino liqueur.

Strawberries with Cream

Wash and remove the stems from some fresh strawberries. Sprinkle them with sugar, then cover them with heavy cream whipped up with sugar and a tiny bit of port or cognac.

Chestnut Cream

Make some sweetened chestnut puree. Here's how: Mix 2 generous tablespoons chestnut flour with 1 generous tablespoon sugar. Add a package of vanilla sugar. Add enough milk to make a mixture that is just barely liquid. Put it on the stove and stir constantly. The puree will thicken and begin to swell; add more milk if it's too thick, but be careful. You don't want it to be runny. Cook the puree 3 minutes, then pour it into a dish and let it cool off. When ready to serve, beat some farmer's cheese or soft cream cheese with some heavy cream and a little sugar, and pour it over the chestnut puree.

This is a wonderful dessert, made in almost no time at all. It is the triumph of ten-minute cooking.